Overcoming the Underhanded:

The True Story of a Life Reclaimed

Suzan E. Zan

Overcoming the Underhanded:
The True Story of a Life Reclaimed

Second Edition

ISBN-13: 978-0-9976684-2-1

First Printing: 2016
978-0-9976684-1-4

Table of Contents

Acknowledgments

To my beautiful children who inspire me to be more than I ever thought I could, thank you for your love, your hugs, and for being you.

To my parents Roger and Judy, thank you for your unconditional love and support.

To dear friends Lisa, Carolyn, and David for your encouragement and belief that I can and should write my story; Beth, for your guiding insight, and safe house; author Faith, for your heart and desire to help make this book known.

To therapists Sheila, Kim, Erik, Andrea, Ernie, thank you for your comfy couches and for listening and advocating for our well-being.

To my accomplished bulldog of a lawyer, Mitch, for sticking with me against the bully and for being patient with payment.

To all of our family and friends and the legions of angels that loved on us and prayed for us, God bless you.

Finally, humble thanks to God for not only seeing us through the storm but allowing me this journey that taught me to trust in Him.

Foreword

Authentic love does not devalue, devastate, or play on another's insecurities, and fear and intimidation are not reasons to stay in a relationship.

Any relationship. Especially not a marriage.

My marriage was far from authentic or ideal.

I have the personal journal pages to prove it.

I begin my story when I first met Ahmet, a dashing young man from southern Turkey. It was a fairy tale romance at first, and then turned quite nightmarish as years progressed.

I stood by my man just shy of 15 years until we began to unravel faster than a Persian rug purchased at a flea market.

A third-person synopsis is simple enough:

Husband drunk...husband angry...husband lashes out at wife...wife afraid, cries...husband sleeps it off, acts like it never happened...wife walks on egg shells, disengages from the marriage...husband says he's sorry/gets angry at wife for "making him this way"...wife makes excuses for husband's behavior...puts up a brave front for kids...repeat.

It reads like a tragedy that fills up a lot of my journal pages—different day, different year, same story.

The questions of why I was vulnerable and allowed myself to fall victim to such bad treatment can complete a whole other book. This book starts with me outrageously tired—emotionally, physically, mentally.

It was time to move on.

More than time.

It was seriously long overdue.

I was done.

Over.

Overdone.

Ahmet always said I should write our story one day.

I'm quite sure this isn't the story he had in mind for me to tell but I must tell it.

My intent is not to bash him, men in general, marriage, the Middle East, or Muslims for that matter. I hope it encourages conversation to confront the uncomfortable and serves as an inspiration to leave a bad situation for a brighter future. Sometimes your gut kicks in and lets you know the unknown has got to be better than where you are.

This is my story.

Chapter One

Damn Ladies Night

Question:
What should you do if a foreign guy sweeps you out onto the dance floor, is very drunk, and says he wants to go out with you?
Answer:
Run, and do not give him your phone number!

It was nearly 10 p.m. Thursday night at Club X and it was "Ladies Night."

I remember it well. I can still smell the noxious mixture of cigarettes, beer, rum, and God knows what else that molded into the shabby garnet carpet. Odors of heavy cologne and perfumed people couldn't mask that smell.

I was at the modestly decorated night club after work with three of my female besties and my bestie guy friend Larry. Larry would have loved to be my best boyfriend but I just didn't feel that way. There was no chemistry, just friendship. Plus, his brother alluded to an addiction to strip clubs...no thank you!

I came to Club R to dance and have a few drinks with my friends. It was a nice place that fit the "after-college-no-more-frat-houses" scene without breaking the bank, especially on Ladies Night. I liked to get out and socialize, be seen on the scene, but I wasn't looking

1

to meet or "hook up" with anyone.

I know a lot of women say that when they really have an ulterior motive and are looking for Mr. Right or Mr. Right Now. But I wasn't.

It was 1992, two years after college and I was gainfully employed full time (no small feat for those depressed times). It had been more than a year since my last failed relationship and I still wasn't in a place where I desired to land a boyfriend. I found celibacy looked good on me and was starting to enjoy not having any relationship entanglements.

While dancing to *The Cure* (or maybe it was *Nine Inch Nails?)* I bumped into a grinning 6'1" dark-haired, well-dressed man with an alluring smile. We danced next to one another for a while and he was soon annoyingly encroaching my personal space.

Ah, but he was nice looking. Well put together—so not like an awkward college boy who thinks he's a big shot if he orders wine.

If memory recalls correctly I spoke first to break the silence of his unnerving stare.

Damn, why'd I do that?

"What's your name?" I yelled over the suddenly-too-loud music.

To this day I'm not quite sure what he replied. It wasn't a name I was familiar with for sure.

Why is that music so loud?

I asked him again and threw in a "how old are you?" because he looked a fair amount older than I.

The next song that played allowed me to hear his heavy accent clearer, but continued to help mask his intoxication.

He smiled when he said his name was Ahmet but then proceeded to tell me where he lived instead of revealing his age.

What accent is this?

Almost as soon as we started talking, several other dark-haired men seemed to be giving him "the nod." He was here at Ladies Night with friends too, and I learned later they were all from Turkey. I had never met anyone from that country before. Heck, not like I knew too many people from any other country for that matter. They sure were enjoying themselves, whooping it up loudly, proudly prancing on the crimson-speckled dance floor with drinks in hand.

After another song started, Ahmet came in a little too close and tried to plant one on me. Whoa, then I smelled the alcohol on his breath!

I excused myself to say that I had to get up early for work the next morning and needed to get going, "nice meeting you, bye."

I gathered my gang who could tell by reading my face that I wanted to leave. But what do girls do? We first use the ladies room before the drive home because, you know, you never know.

Why did you use the bathroom before leaving...?

When I exited the bathroom there he was with a huge smirk on his handsome face. He said it was destiny as he thought I had left, and could he please have my number.

Damn.

I floundered some but was, of course, flattered.

He was very nice looking, well dressed, clean shaven, and smelled slightly of lemons. I was well aware he was drunk and thought no harm in giving him my work number.

"He'll never in a million years hang onto my number or remember our encounter," I speculated.

Crap. I was wrong.

Chapter Two

The Persistent Peacock

Google "facts about Turkish men" and nearly every website will describe them as persistent.

I know this now.

Google, where were you in 1992!

Ahmet most certainly did not lose my number as I surmised he would. He freaked me out when he first called me at work—then every day for four days asking if I'd go out with him. I have to admit his persistence was flattering and caught me off guard as previous men I had dated didn't have that "go-getter-gumption" quality to them.

After several days of trying to get me to go out, I found myself agreeing to meet with him for dinner on a Wednesday night, much to the dismay of my boss. Karen instantly had reservations about Ahmet as I described our meeting and his nationality. She thought there was an ulterior motive to his persistence.

Gee, thanks. Maybe it's because a boyfriend would distract me from working too hard for you?

"Heck, it's a Wednesday, not a weekend which barely makes it a date," I told her.

I wanted to meet at the restaurant we discussed since I didn't want him (or any man at this stage) to know where I lived. A single girl in the city can never be too careful. But he persisted, got me a little confused and flustered by changing the plans a few times, and smooth-talked me right out of that self-protective notion. Ahmet picked me up promptly at 7 p.m.

Now I want to state that I am very much a structured, yet outgoing, earthy, Virgo girl, and flexibility is just a natural part of my DNA. God programmed me to be agreeable and accommodating— although I'm quite certain my parents felt I was anything but accommodating when I was 15 and knew it all.

Heck, find me a teenage girl that doesn't have a dose of demon in her and I'll shine her halo myself!

Word to the wise: While these traits may make you likable, be sure you know who YOU are and what you stand for. While I had never considered myself "submissive" or "weak," my happy-go-lucky personality secured Ahmet's position in the driver's seat. Of course, couple that with Turkish male bravado and well, you'll see.

My requests, wishes, dreams, demands, or whatever, would continue to take the backseat throughout our future relationship. I was putty being molded by a manipulative mastermind.

Chapter Three

Hold on for a Magic Carpet Ride

Back when I was still warm and fuzzy about our relationship, I used to tell people that Ahmet and I had a magical first date, that I really thought the lightning bolt had stuck.

Something struck me, all right—slow daggers to my self-esteem and well-being…

Aside from the slight language barrier, we talked for hours that first night together. Actually, I think it was just Ahmet that talked. He shared that he was from a small city in southern Turkey. He had only been in the United States for about six months and was taking English classes at night at the local university. His American adventure began a week after his Turkish army service ended. His uncle offered him the chance to come to Florida to help run his business. Ahmet was the oldest of three children and he spoke so lovingly of his whole family, I was mesmerized.

I'd never learned so much about a guy on the first date. Hell, I'd been in a few long-term relationships and knew less about the guy—so much information had been shared! He was so forthright, so full of energy, so alive! Ahmet certainly liked to talk and this communicative Virgo found that an admirable trait.

Sucker. What about listening skills or taking turns with conversation? Duh, communication is a two-way street!

Ahmet was what I called three E's: Enthusiastic, Exciting, and Exotic. His middle-eastern culture intrigued me. He was unlike any other young man I'd dated from my "typical" middle-American class life. Even his smell was captivating, *Limon Kolonyasi*, or better known as lemon cologne.

I was swept off my feet and we were soon inseparable. Ahmet was hard-working and ambitious.

And he was a liar from the start. I see that looking back.

Getting an evasive answer when I asked where he lived should have been my first clue. Turns out he was shacked up with some woman who had a dog and he didn't like pets (another sign—animals are very in-tune to personalities!). Was she just his roommate or someone he grew tired of? I'll never know, but if it were just a living arrangement, why lie about it?

That was the first lie. I think. More than once I'd find him floundering around with words, often he'd manage to tie it up all nicely, excusing it away, until it seemed I was the one making an issue out of nothing. And in the grand scheme of things, I believed no real harm was being done.

So gullible to the gaslighting that was going down.

Chapter Four

Slice of Reality...Check!

About a year into our relationship, I realized I had pretty much abandoned the people I regularly hung out with—these previous friendships included both male and female. Gone were my besties. There was always something Ahmet complained about and he just didn't think my friends *"were quality people."*

His one exception was my single gal-pal, Kat. He seemed to adore her and she him. Any previously-held male friends were given the third degree four times over, again, and again.

I tried to assure Ahmet that he was now my *"one and only"* but he was very jealous and didn't believe a man and woman could just be friends and nothing more. I tried to keep in touch with my guy friends, but it became so bad that I just stopped asking to spend time with them because of the fight I knew I'd have with Ahmet if I tried.

Spending time with Turkish friends however, was always allowed and it seemed that became our only social circle. Turkish men who drank and grilled mega amounts of meat—it was a favorite cultural pastime—eating and drinking and shooting the shit. The trouble was the shit being spoken was all in Turkish, which I was picking up rather easily.

I must take a moment to brag and give myself some credit. I never knew I had talent to pick up a

9

foreign language, but something about it clicked within me and I was great at mimicking the sounds back. My vocabulary was swelling like a camel's hump.

I was a natural and took pride in this, yet I wasn't, nor am I now fluent in Turkish by any means. If you've ever been part of a conversation or have been at a gathering where you don't speak the language, you know the joy it is being the odd one out. You're physically present for the conversation but feel like a ghostly outsider especially when everyone busts out laughing hysterically and you never knew a punchline was coming.

"What's the joke? What's so funny? Please translate..." gets old quickly—so does the fact that you've been tuned out and are being rudely ignored by your date. *For hours!*

So, what do you do?

You sit.

You smile.

You sulk.

You eat or drink too much.

You use the fricken' bathroom even when you don't have to go just for something to do. And you watch the clock out of boredom while others party like it's 1999 (or is it 2099 now?).

I came to detest "Turks grill night" yet I bet if you polled the five young immigrants that regularly gathered, these men would call it the best time of their lives.

I understood their bond to each other and empathized that they were homesick and missed their family and country.

But did they have to drink like the next oasis was 1,000 miles away?

Ahmet had a huge tolerance for alcohol. I was a lightweight with a weak stomach. I don't like to drink that much, never have.

God is smiling down right now saying, *"Good, she finally learned after many nights worshipping the porcelain 'me' in school!"*

I could have one or two drinks, maybe three over a stretch of time, but why? It never settled right in my stomach. Here was a man, my boyfriend telling me I "needed to relax" and I should have several drinks to do it.

Peer pressure to drink from my boyfriend, seriously?!

One crisp autumn night, we went out to dinner at a Chinese buffet just the two of us. He had several drinks as well as several plates of food. In addition to drinking in bulk, Ahmet was also quite the bulk eater. He could skip meals but then sure pack it on in one sitting. I actually preferred his eating habits over his drinking habits since I didn't mind eating or eating out.

I enjoy eating. I'll admit it. I've been a curvy size 14/16 for most of my life and while I've never been happy with my weight, I came to understand "I am how I am" unless I decide to make some changes for myself.

Like quitting smoking.

I did that on my own but only when I was ready.

For as long as I can remember I've been prone to food cravings. I rarely ever planned on what to eat because I was never sure what I'd be in the mood for the next day. Italian, Mexican, Chinese, a hot dog…it's leveled off as I've gotten older and learned to control it better. But food and I go way *weigh* [sic] back.

On that particular Saturday night, I had suggested an Asian buffet place we both liked. One, it was cheap, and two, the food was real good. He happily agreed and we both devoured more food than we should have.

That is the true nature of the American buffet, right?

As Ahmet drove us home he became agitated. I don't know maybe his already snug fitting European jeans were too tight. I wasn't sure what caused his sudden sour mood until he blurted that we "pigged out" and it was my fault!

The next words he said are forever etched in my brain, "The reason why we have 'little sex' is that you're fat and disgust me."

Oh my God did I hear him right?

Never in a million years did I see that hateful, hurtful statement coming—from someone who supposedly loved me.

I was too shocked to speak. I'm not even sure if I uttered a word before my eyes welled with an ocean of stabbing pain. I ran away from him when he dropped me off, then proceeded to cry hysterically until I ended up puking up my pork lo mein. I cried a thousand tears, moped around for days, and didn't see him for a week.

Putting some distance between us had an effect on him and he began to profess how sorry he was for saying that. He said his mother scolded him too. Good, she should have. Photos of his family certainly looked as if they never missed a meal either.

My mother wanted to kill him. It was the first of many times...

Ahmet lamely said he was trying to be motivating and encourage me since he knew I wasn't happy with my weight.

Oh, that was smooth and a nice touch, don't you agree?

So what did I do?

Forgave him.

Chapter Five

What's a Green Card Got to Do with It?

"I need to go back home. My sister wants to get married," said Ahmet.

His sister, Aleyna, the middle child, had been dating a nice Turkish guy for more than a year. He was educated, had a good job and was what Ahmet referred to as a "good Muslim" meaning he didn't drink, smoke, and he honored the fast during Ramadan—unlike himself.

"That's great news," I said.

Yet as Ahmet's bushy eyebrows fused into one, I could see he wasn't happy.

"I have to stop their marriage," he blurted.

"Why? I thought he was a great guy," I said, confused.

"Because he is from Arabic background and I'm the man of the house."

Ahmet's father had died some years before and even though he was in the United States he was expected to fulfill his patriarchal duties. His uncles did not approve of the marriage because they looked down on Arabs—even Turkish ones.

My lack of knowledge on Middle Eastern culture showed, for I did not grasp he was serious about two things: first, not approving the marriage, and second, leaving the country.

"Why? This guy was born and raised in Turkey—how is he not considered suitable?"

Here I was, this American New York girl, deeply involved with Ahmet—and they were accepting of *our* relationship but not his sister's?

I didn't get it. Still don't. What I finally got was that Ahmet had to leave America and go back to Turkey and with only a student Visa about to expire; it was unclear if he would be allowed to return to the U.S.

Chapter Six

Come Get Me

Within no time at all, Ahmet made his preparations to return home. He offered for me to go with him, promising that it would be a beautiful adventure.

I told him I'd had the opportunity to visit England and Amsterdam before and they were about as close to American culture as you can get and I didn't want to live in those countries either.

The U.S. was my home and I was not going to give it up. Not even for him.

Our goodbye at the airport played like a scene from a love-struck romance movie…man and woman embracing as if they'd shatter if separated…tears flowing freely. Time seemed to stand still as we slowly parted, neither knowing if this was the end of our relationship. All that was known at the time was that it would be a long time before we saw each other again.

Or even if we did.

The large international airport was strangely calm with few travelers hustling about. I was thankful for the relative quietness. I also appreciated that my tear-streaked face wasn't seen by many as I made the long walk out of the airport alone. With each step, I gained some comfort for I knew in my heart I wasn't meant to give up everything and uproot my life to move to Turkey—even though I loved him and wanted it to work out.

At least I got that part right...

He called me when he arrived at his city and said he was excited to see his family again.

I'll never know what transpired back in his home country but just four short days later he started the conversation by saying, "Suzan, my life is nothing without you. There's nothing here for me in Turkey. Come get me."

Come get me. What did that mean? Get married? Have a life together? Was that a marriage proposal?

He used those words to put me in motion to help bring him back in the United States—for good.

Or so he said.

Ahmet approved of his sister's choice to marry Burak after all, and they were to be wed in April, which was three months away. I was to begin planning our own wedding, travel to Turkey (by myself), meet his entire family, attend the wedding, then come back with Ahmet and get married in two weeks.

Travel to Turkey by myself?

I was such a naïve 22-year-old who didn't fully comprehend the ramifications of such an international escapade. I saw this only as a worldly romantic adventure. Looking back now I give my parents a lot of credit for remaining calm and not having me committed after I told them what was happening.

For the record, I'll be locking my daughter in her room indefinitely if she tries to do anything like I did!

With a wedding to plan in three mere months, time passed quickly. My mom, the proverbial planner, has an innate talent for details and entertaining. She researched her heart out and we kept it as simple as possible. Still, for a wedding you need a venue, invitations, food, flowers, something to wear, and such.

At least we only needed one venue, since we were not going to be married in a church, per Ahmet's religious beliefs. This didn't bother me because, although I was Christian, I did not have a church home or go to church regularly.

I'm sure this quick, get married, shot-gun type of wedding (and no, the bride wasn't pregnant) wasn't how my parents thought my "special day" would or should go, but they were troopers. I was just elated to be getting married.

Finally, I'm 23 already!

My boss thought I was crazy as did some of my peers, but I took two weeks of absence from work to go get my groom. In April, I boldly travelled alone to a southern region in Turkey—a journey that required four planes (at the time) to get there!

I was crazy in love and felt confident I was doing the right thing. Changing planes in Istanbul proved slightly scary. My connecting fourth flight was at a terminal far, far away. I never would have known this if it weren't for a friendly thirtysomething German-Turkish woman who spoke flawless English. Thank

God for her. She grabbed my hand as we exited the plane and told me to keep my eyes downcast as the men would surely soak up my green eyes.

As I stole quick glances about, I had never before seen such similarity in physical traits as I did once past the gate! Everywhere I looked I saw men with hair as dark as coal. My totally unnatural blond hair had me feeling like a penguin in a forest. I felt a firm hand on me as she pulled me closer to her. One guy lunged forward to grab me!

This is absolutely wild...I am nearly invisible in my own country.

I mean, I think I am pretty decent looking, and my eyes are an amazing greenish blue, but I'm not a head-turner nor have I ever felt a spotlight on me.

Ah, but in Turkey I stood out.

More than that, I was welcomed with a warmth I never expected, not in my wildest dreams. From his mom to his sister and brother, aunts and uncles, and a gazillion cousins—everyone I met was passionately social and affectionate and a little in awe of me, this young woman who had travelled 10 plus hours, four planes, and ventured across the seas to meet them.

I was a rock star!

All of Ahmet's relatives seemed to readily accept me as a bride for him from the moment I touched down on their soil. Well, all but one aunt. I didn't have to speak fluent Turkish to sense her hostility to me. When I questioned my fiancé about it later it turns out I was correct in diagnosing her abrasive cold shoulder.

Seems she had envisioned her daughter marrying Ahmet.

Um, she's your cousin...first cousin at that. Gross!

That should have been my clue to realize that his family wasn't as "European" or "modern" as Ahmet said they were.

Chapter Seven

Repeat After Me, You're Muslim Now

Question:
If you are deceived into renouncing your religion does it count?
Answer:
Only against the deceiver.

Aleyna and Burak's wedding was elegant and beautiful and I was awestruck to be the American girl with a front-row view to it all. I found that Americans share many of the same wedding traditions as Turks do to celebrate a couple's union. Aleyna had primped and been wonderfully pampered before the wedding, much like an American bride. I was able to join her as well, receiving a full cosmetic makeover and hair styling complete with using hot hairbrushes as a curling iron.

The bride was exquisitely made up and was stunning in her white, floor-length gown. Burak was handsome in his dark suit and they entered the flower-filled rented ballroom together, much to my surprise (but this was normal for their custom).

They were brought to a head table facing their guests and a brief service was conducted so they could sign the official documents declaring them husband and wife. The couple then made their way around the room, and they were given money. Gold coins tied with tiny red silk bows were pinned on the new bride. Traditional gifts for the bride and groom are money and gold.

No toasters or towels for these newlyweds!

Then came the food, courses and courses of flavorful dishes—some of which I enjoyed; some of it I played with on my plate so as not to appear rude. The cake was an amazing five layers high—I sure didn't envy the person who had to transport that to this venue!

Traditional and modern music was played by a live orchestra, and dancing ensued well throughout the night. All in all, it was a celebration very much like a traditional American wedding.

Except for the fact that it was all spoken in Turkish and my one translator was out-of-pocket playing big brother/father-of-the-bride.

A few days after the wedding, Ahmet said his family wanted to throw us a modest engagement party before we left, since no one would be able to come to our wedding ceremony in the United States.

While my future husband was not a "practicing" Muslim, he explained how being a Muslim was very important to his family.

He told me they wanted to take me to meet with a religious man who would explain more about Islam, since it was very important that I pledge to accept Ahmet as a Muslim and promise to learn more about his religion.

Ahmet knew exactly what to say so I wouldn't protest or be the wiser.

His statements sounded fine to me. Of course I would accept him and his religion, I was going to marry him, wasn't I? I loved learning new things and I found his culture captivating.

Never did I suspect I was being tricked into renouncing my religion and converting to Islam.

Even though I didn't go to church, I'm a Christian and I believe that Jesus is the son of God and my salvation is through Him.

The morning I was to meet with the religious man, I was told to bathe three times. My clothes were to be modest, covering my arms and legs, and I was to wear one of his mother's headscarves to cover my hair.

I know, I know, these were clues and I should have guessed it.

Ah, but I was enthralled by the excitement and mystique of it all and I didn't piece the dots together in my innocence. I just remember feeling as if I were a princess in a fairy tale in a faraway land.

Aren't fairy tales always a little too good to be true?

Both his mom and his favorite aunt accompanied us to the mosque and I knew something was amiss when I was asked to repeat something three times.

There's a pattern of three's here...

Turns out I was asked to recite the Testimony of Faith (Shahada), which is pronounced as:

"La ilaha illa Allah, Muhammad rasoolu Allah."

Translated, these Arabic words mean, "There is no true god but Allah, and Muhammad is the Messenger (Prophet) of God."

(But I was never told that at the time.)

It's no wonder Ahmet didn't tell me that I was going through the motions of converting to Islam. He knew if he asked me that I wouldn't have renounced my faith. Even though I was not strong in my faith, I still felt strongly about God and Jesus Christ.

To not go through with his family's request (heck, it might have been a conditional demand on their part—I'll never know) would have caused him great embarrassment since it would signify that I was not willing to submit to my husband. And it could have been potentially dangerous for me, I suppose, being in a predominantly Muslim country.

Regardless, it's neither here nor there because he lied to get me to do it and it doesn't count. My gesture made his family happy and we had our engagement party just before we left to go back to America.

Like my future sister-in-law, I too, was showered with jewelry and gold coins.

Granted, it could've been payment to sell me off at the black market, heck what did I know back then?

But how could anyone not think it all a dream?

I didn't realize at the time that I was being tricked. I was swept up in the romantic fantasy of it all and grossly overlooked this critical sign of foreboding.

He had blatantly lied and deceived me.

Chapter Eight

Signs, Signs, Everywhere

Having a mere three months to plan a marriage was like hitting the turbo button on a Super Mario Bros™ game. Once we returned from Turkey, the countdown to marital bliss was T minus two weeks.

Ahmet had given me free reign of making all wedding decisions, and I eagerly shared that power with my mom because let's face it, I didn't know what to do. But mom did and she excels at details while I detest them. Maybe detest is too strong a word but I clearly didn't realize how much was involved and how many decisions there were to make.

It would be a simple, smallish affair with some close friends and some dear family flying in from New York. My brother and my best friend, Kat, were to be our best man and maid of honor.

No one from Ahmet's family was coming to our wedding. Not his mom, brother, sister, uncles...no one. At the last minute, his best friend, Kemal, decided he'd come down and be there for his buddy. Kemal was attending a university in Pennsylvania at the time and he, too, had met a nice American girl. Yet he wasn't sure he should marry her.

Was I really sure? Is anyone ever?

I knew I had missed him when he went back to Turkey but I wasn't willing to sacrifice myself to move there. If I were truly in love, shouldn't I have? And what about Ahmet?

Had he given it enough time and thought to what a commitment we were making together?

All questions that should have been asked.

Regardless, plans were in motion and I was happy that he would have some "family" in attendance. My mom quickly sewed another bridesmaid's dress after my cousin was kind enough to join in the happy day.

The night before the wedding Kat, Kemal, Ahmet, and I had dinner together before splitting off. The boys partied (and who knows what else) until the sun came up while Kat and I quietly retreated to her apartment for girl talk.

I can't say that I was having true pre-jitters, but I remember feeling numb; going through the motions and all the steps but feeling emotionless.

Shouldn't I be ecstatic to be spending the rest of my life with the man I loved?

Sign.

The next day was a comedy of errors starting with our hair appointments at a place in the nearby mall. My hair came out lovely and I was pleased. Kat told the lady she didn't want her below-the-chin-length hair too poufy and well, I can freely admit it now that she did kind of look like Roseanne Roseannadanna from Saturday Night Live when the lady was finished.

Kat was so pissed and was not about to go anywhere looking like that. She insisted we go back to her place, so she could shower and redo her hair. This made us late since we had to go about 15 miles on a hellish highway to get to my wedding venue. I was upset that she was willing to make me late for my own wedding just so she could have good hair.

Sign?

To top it all off, a mini tropical storm decided to descend upon us on that very day. It was a downpour of all downpours that May day, and the highway was backed up beyond belief, because Florida drivers do not know how to drive in the rain.

We were a good 30 minutes past the time I should have arrived. This was 1993, pre-cell phone days, so I had no way of getting word to my parents or the wedding party that we were on our way. Stopping at a pay phone would've put us even more behind schedule.

I would come to find out that my family thought we were in a tragic accident along I-4; not that I bolted, which would have been the smarter choice. The torrential rain swept away our beautiful blueprint for our outside, lakeside marriage at sunset. It was now on to plan B; move the wedding inside the club house's small ballroom.

Sign.

Oops, they forgot to leave enough space for two people who weren't size fours to walk down the aisle. Not leaving ample room for the bride and her father to walk down was cause enough for heart palpitations, but something even more tragic occurred. Just as my dad and I were making our first steps, the cameraman I hired (colleague's partner) whispered that the camera we had paid for him to rent was locked and he didn't know how to open it.

So that meant there would be no professional photos.

Are you kidding me?

It was the cherry on top of an already botched day.

But we got in front of the Justice of the Peace (no man of God in respect of the groom's religion) and were quickly married. The ceremony was seriously short once you take out almost all references to religion.

"Speak now or forever hold your peace."

Pause...pause...no one? Really? Ok. Let's do it.

We were pronounced man and wife and whew, that part was over.

My relatives and other adults all did their best to snap as many photos as they could to help commemorate our day but it just didn't make up for professional photos. My husband would later blame me for being cheap and using a 'gay' to photograph such an important event.

Sign.

The rest of the night is really a blurred memory as it whirled by so fast. It's amazing how rapidly that day really goes when you're in the moment. All the plans, all the details, all for a very short time frame...

How do people stand planning for six months to a year and to have it all be over in a few short hours?

I don't remember seeing Ahmet drink that much that night but his eyes told a much different story. And actually, he confessed to me later that he had just basically continued the drinking from the previous night, never really sobering up.

I do remember getting to our hotel by limousine, which my parents paid for both, and him being ravenously hungry. The marriage was consummated, um, very quickly. He ordered a pizza from room service and passed out after a slice, leaving me awake and alone. It was barely 11 p.m.

Yeah, it was a great way to start married life.

Chapter Nine

Marriage Was No Turkish Delight

Marriage to Ahmet was…
Unpredictable…
Off-balance…
Frustrating…
Normal at times…
Roller-coaster like…
Hard to describe for sure…
Interesting to say the least.

About nine years into our marriage, Ahmet and I briefly separated—his decision, then mine. Let me explain.

With our children, Nikole and Tarik, four and two respectively, I went back to work full time. A great job opportunity at a worldwide corporation presented itself to me and I just couldn't pass it up. It was the real deal. Beautiful five-star four-story building; modern yet comfy office furniture; eclectic and creative management; and I even got an ID badge. I had forgotten how exciting a job could be.

You see, when our daughter was born Ahmet made it very clear that he preferred me to stay home with her. "You should enjoy raising her, cleaning the home, and preparing home-cooked meals—most women would kill for this chance," he said.

Plus, he loved to remind me that I wasn't making that much money since I wasn't a manager like he was.

We also didn't have any family close by to help out and with child care costs being what they were. Besides, Ahmet's career in cars was taking off and his salary could adequately provide for the three of us.

It was his "duty" as the man, he said.

So, although I had loved my job, I agreed with his reasoning and quit, or as I liked to say, *"took a work hiatus"* to raise our daughter.

Then 18-months later, we were blessed with the arrival of our son. That made for two babies under two years old, both in diapers and requiring daycare if I went back to work. Financially, it just made sense to remain at home. Although it also hurled me into the traditional "dutiful" role that eradicated my voice and "vote" as time passed.

Don't get me wrong. I adored my babies. They were my world. They made my life bearable. And while I loved being a stay-at-home mom for nearly four years, the chance to be back around professional adults had me feeling super-dee-dooper excited!

"I love you. You love me. We're a happy family."

Ahhh, make it stop…

WAY too much Barney back then!

I took the job which fit nicely within my college degree skillset, marketing and communications, and although Ahmet was fond of the money I was now making (in addition to the health coverage we had with me employed), he was not a fan of my growing independence.

I wouldn't argue over money per se, I just

questioned why our bank account didn't reflect that we were getting ahead as we should be now that I was working too. He did not take kindly to me questioning our finances—or my new desire to get out of the house more.

In the year I had been with the company, I decided to join my team after work for happy hour. I'd been asked before but it never seemed the right time. This instance was literally the only time I went with them to grab some cold beers and hot wings. I was out for two hours after work and it felt great to socialize with my peers.

When I got home, he was furious.

I'm not sure what brought it on. Maybe the kids had been difficult? Two toddlers requiring attention and work, imagine that?

Threatening to "divorce my pathetic ass" was nothing new to my ears, as he'd said this to me many times before. He especially loved to tell me this when he was having a "rough time" at work, which to me, felt often. Ahmet was never, ever satisfied with what he had accomplished by working here in America. He came to this country with one suitcase and me—and together we had made quite a nice life for ourselves.

But he never felt like it was enough and he'd always lament that we "could have better if we lived in Turkey." His idea/dream/fantasy/escape plan was to take out a home equity loan, max out our credit cards, and leave the United States to live in Turkey like "kings" where he was "a god."

If he thought he was a king there why didn't he

stay in Turkey?

I can't remember how many times we fought over which country to live in. For me, it was a non-negotiable. He knew that going into our marriage that I did not want to live in Turkey…and now we had babies to consider!

As much as I loved his family, I did not think I would be happy there. Whether you consider Turkey more European or more Middle Eastern, one thing is without argument—it is not America, home of the free and the brave.

That night Ahmet again exclaimed he should divorce me and find someone better. Maybe it was the two beers I had consumed that provoked my sudden outburst of courage, but I answered, "You know what? Go ahead, go for it. I'm done too!"

Much to his surprise, I actually meant it as much as he did.

Maybe even more.

Chapter Ten

Partner or Possession?

My husband had a temper.

Everyone does, myself included.

On more than one occasion I've been known to curse, punch a pillow, light a cigarette (back in the day), and take breaths so deep my lungs would nearly explode.

Or was that after inhaling?

Ahmet, on the other hand, clearly did not learn good anger management skills growing up. Sure, he was easygoing with everyone else, but to the kids and me he was critical and sarcastic—especially when we were alone.

My husband was a great storyteller, an entertainer almost, and he could reel you in with his charm and flare for the dramatic, dangling his hook with a plausible tale. If I said something that questioned or contradicted whatever perfect story he was spinning, I'd catch hell when alone.

Maybe I had crossed the line a few times. Hell, I know I'm not perfect. I admit I have issues with wanting to be liked and included. Ah, but there were times I didn't even realize that the line was drawn and he'd turn on me with very little warning. The conversation would be fine one moment and then *BOOM.* It felt like he just wanted me to go along and play the dutiful wife, maintain the happy façade that he was king and I was his loving queen.

But after hearing his lips utter that he wanted a divorce enough times, I began to evaluate that possibility as an actual option.

If he's miserable and I'm miserable, why are we staying married? Is it just for the kids?

Although Nikole and Tarik were two great reasons I knew it wasn't going to be enough to hold us together.

So, Ahmet packed a bag and left for a few nights while I remained home and began bracing myself to be a single mom of two in Pre-K. I cried a lot, vented to my mom and dad a lot, and was in disbelief that we were really over.

Yet during this time I also felt the beginnings of calm as I cared for my kids without his unpredictable influence. They didn't understand what was happening and both kids were becoming tense not hearing from *Baba* [Turkish for father], but my resolve was brewing inside of me that this decision was for the best.

I'm not exactly sure of his trigger, but after a few days of freedom, Ahmet had a change of heart and said he was sorry and wanted his family back.

He tried to win me over by taking me out to talk one night, just us. He bought me flowers, took us to a nice dinner, the whole nine yards, trying to woo me as he had when we first started dating.

I wasn't buying it. I'd heard the "I'm sorry" before. And flowers and gifts and dinners out don't mean that you're loved.

I was starting to feel like it was just because it

was "cheaper to keep her" and not because of any real love he had for me.

If he loved us so much, why did he spend so much time away from us?

Work aside, even when home Ahmet would retreat to the back patio with a drink to watch sports; or he'd invite more Turkish kids over to party with him. I say kids because he loved playing the *abi* [Turkish for older brother] to young single males; never did he seem interested in finding married couples to develop a friendship with.

I must have completely thrown him off guard when I said, "No, I think we really should divorce. You're obviously not happy; you never want to spend time with me or the kids; and you're drinking way too much. This is hard but it's for the best."

He was enraged like I'd never seen him before—and I'd seen him get pissed off ugly. He accused me of all sorts of things, most of all "Who's the guy you're screwing?"

He also tried to blame me for not letting him know how bad it was getting.

Really? You're drinking too much is my fault now?!

Then Ahmet said the unthinkable and I'll never forget the look in his bloodshot eyes.

He said, "You know how smart I am, right? You know how many friends I have both here and in Turkey. If you don't come back to me, I'll take those kids to Turkey so fast…you know you'll never ever find them or see them again."

36

That did it.

Nikole and Tarik were just so young, so trusting, so portable at the time. Losing them was my deepest rooted fear unearthed.

Call me cowardly, but I guess I wasn't ready for the fight of my life at that time. Ahmet had pleaded with my dad for his help and appeared unannounced one morning, making a grand show and apologizing to me in front of my parents, begging forgiveness. He also presented me with a spectacular diamond and sapphire necklace and he gave the matching earrings to my mother.

Aside from being showered in gold at our engagement, it was only the second time he had bought me jewelry. There was no gesture for giving him a daughter, but when my son was born it was a different story.

(You'll hear more about that later.)

I didn't care squat about the jewelry, although it was truly stunning and must have cost us a pretty penny. I was more touched by the fact that he finally agreed that we should see a marriage counselor. We did actually go—twice.

After just two visits it became a hassle to schedule and he said he was being "ganged up on" because the therapist was on my side. Ironically, it was Ahmet who had picked the middle-aged male counselor.

"Don't worry, we're good," he said. "We love each other, have two great kids."

I didn't really expect him to accept any wrongdoing on his part. He promised things would be different.

I had doubt in my heart but thought maybe, just maybe, I could better manage him by being a better wife and mother.

Oh yeah, that worked well.

Chapter Eleven

Stick a Fork in Me, I'm Overdone

Question:
Which do you think is worse, knowing that you're stuck in a pit or living stuck in blissful ignorance?
Answer:
It's a trick question. There is no right answer.

Fast forward another six years. Ahmet puts in a lot of hours at work, but it is paying off. We take some mini-vacations. I dive deep into loving my children and getting involved in their lives.

The story doesn't change much, just the days. Ahmet drinks…too much. He lashes out at me when he's in a whiskey-induced tirade and hateful accusatory words flow easily off the tip of his tongue.

When Ahmet wanted to be intimidating he had no problem, since he was 6' 1" and his weight fluctuated between 230-260 pounds. While my "prince charming" had never actually hit me, he certainly could be a mean son-of-a-bitch. Yet on a few occasions, a dinner plate, candle holder, or some household object was thrown at me.

"Sticks and stones may break my bones, but names will never hurt me…"
Bullshit.
They do hurt.

39

And after nearly 15 years of marriage to this man I was becoming an old hag, sad, sagging, and nagging about my plight—my prince a sadistic ruler slowly sucking the life away from "his queen."

I can't remember exactly when or what triggered the thoughts of escaping my marriage (again, but for good). It wasn't really a light-bulb moment, more like the dimmer switch had been on and slowly I had become aware of my ignorance and realized the chains were getting heavier and my life getting darker.

The only real light was my children. They were my world. Nikole and Tarik were two sweet souls, trusting and joyful. They made my life bearable and I focused on them to fill the hole that was painfully obvious in my marriage.

I think that may be why I wanted more children so badly at one point. I kept trying desperately to fill my spiritually empty self.

Ahmet insisted we were done having children once his son arrived, and he elected to have a vasectomy at age 31.

"I can provide better for two children than three or four," he said.

That may very well be true but I still had a yearning to have more children—even though both births were incredibly hard on me.

There was no discussing the matter with Ahmet though. His mind was made up and he made the appointment without regard to how I felt.

Why did I expect anything different?

He made the decisions. He would even make the

decision as to when I should "get rid of things" by randomly throwing out some of my clothes or household items. I'd come home and find he'd "cleaned" and with no regard to personal property, he'd toss items away. He was the man.

A controlling narcissistic man…

I let his doctor know that I wasn't happy about his decision, yet in the end I relented and signed the papers agreeing to the procedure. Lord knows if I dared to embarrass him in the doc's presence I'd have hell to pay.

I hoped I would miraculously get pregnant even after his snip-snip was done. There was a window that made conceiving still possible after all. Yet a voice in the back of my head told me he would accuse me of cheating on him and would probably claim it wasn't his.

That would have been a nightmare all its own.

God saw all that was going on in our marriage and He definitely knew what he was doing by not adding another baby to our mixed-up mayhem. As it was, there would be many times I questioned how and why Ahmet was allowed to be a father.

More than once I found myself seeking solace in my closet—the kids safely tucked in bed, me sobbing while hiding as I'd wait for him to calm down and sober up.

We each had our own closet in our master bedroom and I found it comforting to not only lock the bedroom door but hole up in my own private bunker. Surrounded by boxes of photos, knick-knacks, shoes, and clothes, I felt safe among my stuff. Often, I'd long to leave the house and drive away but I never left him with the kids when he was in that mood.

This was not the way I envisioned spending my nights or life for that matter. In my heart, I knew this was breaking God's heart too and was not a way to live anymore.

But after being beaten down so many times I was now afraid and lacked the strength to stand up for myself.

Our married life wasn't always bad. Truly, it wasn't. There were times of joy.

Yes, sadly just not with him.

Here's my big revelation that was a decade and a half in the making...words of cruelty repeatedly uttered wreck a relationship and deeply damage a soul.

Anyone who is reading please hear me— harmful and hateful words repeatedly ingested is ***mental abuse*** and it can undoubtedly cause a flood of damage.

Chapter Twelve

Release the Tidal Wave of Doubt

As I was nearing the end of my marital rope, I realized I had become more of a possession to Ahmet than a partner. To outsiders we seemed to have a good marriage; but I was growing tired of the façade.

I often joked that I wasn't a single mom but I played one in real life because he was so detached from our daily lives. As a coping mechanism, I detached in my own way and came to dread his days off from work as it surely meant a Bacardi binge and consequent blowout.

We are not ok.

I am not all right.

This is no way to live.

There were so many times I'd pray to God, often from that very same closet I'd hide in, and ask for His guidance and the courage if I should leave Ahmet.

His drinking had become more frequent and intense at home, starting earlier in the day. Quite by accident, I once found economy-sized bottles of rum and whiskey hidden away in our garage already half-consumed.

How do you explain to your husband, who refuses to see he has a drinking problem, who does not treat you with respect, that he's bad for you?

I was slowly coming to the understanding that Ahmet had no desire or belief that things needed to

43

change. It's not a culture or Muslim thing—he was making the choice to not be a good man and the way he talked about and treated people, including me, was depraved.

Now I know it breaks God's heart to see a union end in divorce, but I believe it breaks him even more to see injustices being inflicted.

The fact that I lived with someone that I loved and married someone, who was treating me cruelly, was a gray area of abuse. At least for me it was.

Only an intimate few knew about some of my struggles—my mom and dad, brother, a few very close friends. They had an outside view and could see clearer than I. It's a different story when you're living it daily. For me it was a slow, torturous decent into self-doubt and uncertainty as I faced the truth—it wasn't always bad.

All marriages have their ups and downs, right?

Stepping back, I realize I sounded a lot like a battered wife—justifying and making excuses for his behavior.

"His work is so demanding/he's had a bad day..."
"He doesn't mean it..."
"I shouldn't have pushed the issue..."
"I know better..."

Funny how quickly and easily the third person becomes subjective.

I remember thinking, *"Lord, if he'd just hit me then I'd know for sure I should leave him."*

How tremendously sad is that?

To pray for physical harm so you know you're in the right for leaving…for just wanting out?

It's hard for me to write that one down.

No, once you're at that stage it's safe to say that no amount of couple's therapy can reverse the damage.

Nikole and Tarik were older now, nearing adolescence. They were both smart, observant, and becoming more willful as they were beginning to test their own boundaries as all children do. Ahmet's frequent foul mood and poisonous behavior was becoming harder to keep behind closed doors. And sadly, when they didn't dutifully jump when he asked, or meet up to his "perfect" standards, he started to speak nastily to them, especially our daughter.

I now had company. His wounding words were no longer just aimed at me.

Why did I allow him to bash my self-esteem and fill me with self-doubt just because he wasn't beating me?

Why did I rationalize that "he didn't hurt me" when the truth is he did?

He hurt me time and time again—just not with his fists. And now he was starting on our children…

The telltale signs of physical abuse are brazenly easier to recognize when they are tangible physical evidence. And while bruises and bones heal, it's hard to mend what can't be seen under the surface or in an x-ray.

It's only now, after being divorced a few years and having been in therapy that I am aware of how mentally battered and scarred I was.

Although Nikole was just 11 years old, she was mature beyond her years.

She saw.

She knew.

She experienced his berating too, although I didn't know it at the time for he wielded his words against her in secret. One night after another blowout and her dad passed out on the couch, she snuck over to me and said, "Mom, you deserve to be treated better."

That hit me in the gut.

"Thank you, honey. I agree. We all do."

Chapter Thirteen

Facing the Wild Turkey

Question:
How do you take back control of a life you surrendered?
Answer:
Begin by removing yourself from the chokehold.

Although I knew it was time to start a new life or I would continue to wither like a dried apricot, I took nearly four months to make the decision to end my marriage. It was a gut-wrenching and painfully slow process, one I did not enter lightly. I felt a little selfish I suppose. I'm not really sure if that's the right way to describe it.

How could I do this...to Ahmet...to our children? Do you know how hard it's going to be to start over?

How can I NOT do this? It's not a healthy relationship and it's not good for the kids either.

Tarik, our sensitive and intense son, was already afraid of his dad's Turkish temper and how easily it flared. Secretly, I was more afraid of him becoming just like his old man—thinking it is okay to put women down by threatening and keeping them scared, or badgering, and bullying to get your way.

I knew our kids were old enough that they could see this was not a good marriage. What was almost more agonizing than the realization that it was time to leave was the question of *how* was I going to tell him?

It was a Thursday in October. The kids were settled down for the night.

Was this the right time? Is there ever a good time to turn your life upside down?

In my head I'm thinking: *"We can do this right? Get divorced and be good-natured? After all, it's for the best—neither of us is happy. We have two beautiful children but we just don't work...I wish you happiness, I really do."*

But as for reality, to say he was angry is, well, an understatement.

Shock.

Disbelief.

Drinking.

Anger.

Outrage.

More drinking.

Denial.

More anger.

More drinking.

You get the idea.

It was the longest 10 minutes of my life. (Just kidding.)

This was a conversation that lasted many, many days and carried over like an impending tsunami. As clear as it was to me that we were miserable, Ahmet declared he was oblivious to any problems in our marriage.

He saw nothing wrong with making decisions

regardless of how I felt. Not like he would bother to inquire how I felt. If he wanted it he would not be denied from doing or getting whatever it was. Or he'd lie—and think nothing of it. He also did not agree with the fact that he often treated me bad. Oh, and I overreacted to his drinking and should "lighten up."

Are you kidding me? Oh my God, forget being on the same page—we were not even narrating the same book!

I guess I had distanced myself from the truth that he saw nothing wrong with our life together. If it weren't for our babies, I would have fallen on a sword and not gotten up. My children were my saving grace. It was because of them I found the courage to dig deep when I finally knew I deserved better.

We deserved better.

I thought he would enjoy the opportunity to be single again. It's what he threw in my face so often—to be free.

Whoops. Wrong.

Looking back, I was very naïve (once again) to think he would divorce me amicably.

On the third night, when it was becoming clearer to him that I was serious and not backing down this time, Ahmet's narcissistic arrogance took over. He was shocked and outraged that I would "*dare*" divorce and leave *him*.

That's when the accusations started. Suddenly, I was the whore who must have a lover waiting in the wings...I was cheating on him...I must have had an affair...

After countless, futile times of trying to explain that I hadn't cheated on him, did not have a boyfriend nor was I seeking one, I was simply done, the realization that I was indeed walking away from our marriage must have hit him.

And when it did, it hit him hard and I was clearly caught in the tsunami's inevitable path.

But not in the *"I-love-you-we-can-work-this-out-give-me-another-chance"* kind of way. Rather it was more like:

"What? She's leaving me. How will this look to others—to my family, my work, and my friends? That bitch!"

And that's when it started to get real ugly.

"If you get a lawyer, I swear you'll be sorry," Ahmet warned. *"We split the house 50-50."*

That was fine. I just wanted peace—to not fear the unknown of when the next outburst would come—because it always did.

And each one left me a little more dried up, shattered, and afraid.

Yes, clearly it was time to leave.

Game over.

Chapter Fourteen

What Do I Do Now?

Question:
What is a woman to do when she finds herself up against a high-functioning-alcoholic-narcissist who also happens to be a Turkish Muslim?
Answer:
Find a good lawyer and pray!

In addition to being a master manipulator in our marriage, my husband was without a doubt a gifted salesman. Even after his green card was secured, Ahmet was having trouble finding a job and getting interviews for work. It was my mom who noticed he had a knack for wooing people and she suggested he try sales.

He found his niche shortly after that and started selling pre-loved vehicles within the first year of our marriage. He was an instant success.

Ahmet could sell a car to a blind 90-year-old man who had never driven before and get him to trade up the next year.

He was that good and his paycheck reflected it. We may have started out rocky with my meager salary supporting us, but soon we were able to shed the paycheck-to-paycheck plight and started enjoying "the good life."

Now if you think about it, manipulation and sales go well together since they are a bit similar. It's

Overcoming the Underhanded / Suzan E. Zan

kind of like tea and cookies; they complement each other. To be a manipulator you have to believe in what you're saying or offering to sway the other person toward your view.

And sales, well duh. You have to know your product and be on top of it to talk and sell convincingly.

Please don't hate me if you're reading this and you're a salesperson. I know there are hordes of honest salespeople out there and not everyone's a crook, but come on, let's be real. Whether you're selling real estate, cars, insurance, marketing services, soap or whatever, the salesperson is the one who's highly motivated to make the best deal he or she can to benefit him or herself.

I recalled that Ahmet had a favorite saying about salespeople, "They're all cut from the same mother."

Don't you love the American-Turkish mash-up of proverbial sayings?

That served as a small reminder to me that I would need legal help in separating from this man. Plus, given the real fact that we had two minor children and a home to split, I knew I needed a good lawyer to represent me *(see, I wasn't a total idiot)*.

But I had no clue where to start.

Just accepting the fact that I was leaving this man and a life I had known for nearly 15 years was a lot to digest.

How do I start to look for a lawyer?
Or pay for one.
I was currently unemployed.
Did I mention that yet?

52

I had a job working at Nikole and Tarik's school, but my contract was not renewed for the following year. Yes, I could have tried to find work at a different school but given all that was going unraveling at the home front, I didn't have it in me to try at the time.

This had to take priority.

You know your situation is bad if you're willing to walk away from your marriage and you have nothing to walk on.

For some reason, I wasn't daunted by not having a job; I was increasingly afraid that if I stayed he would suck the life out of all of us.

My family was very supportive of my decision to finally leave Ahmet and thankfully my mom worked with a real estate lawyer, Cynthia, who happily referred me to a lawyer she knew well.

"If I were in a corner, I'd want Adam," Cynthia said. "He's a bulldog."

Having no knowledge of other lawyers and taking comfort in the fact that a personal connection could be made, I quickly and quietly arranged for my free consultation with Adam.

My next-door neighbor and friend, Penny, who also had tween-age children, had taken an interest in helping me. She and her husband were smack in the middle of getting a divorce, as well, and she was putting up quite a fight. I was very appreciative when she offered to drive me to the lawyer's office.

The blonde, perky, petite, fearless, flirtatious, firecracker stayed true to her word and escorted me to meet my potential lawyer late one afternoon. This was a welcomed act of kindness because I was a mess—a complete mess. I was still in disbelief that I was really going through with it. Being in a lawyer's office—I had never been in one before—made my decision to leave him even more real; almost convincing me that I could do this.

Adam strongly encouraged Penny to wait in the lobby so he and I could speak freely. This would later turn out to be a great affirmation that I had indeed selected a wonderful lawyer.

Adam was a bit younger than I and we were about the same height, yet he stood tall with confidence that wasn't egotistical or arrogant. I liked that. I was done with men that felt the need to posture and pump out their chests like, *"Ooh, look up at me, fear me, woman!"*

I don't even think I had uttered a complete sentence before my tears showed up and just wouldn't stop. Adam sat quietly and let me speak. He was a seasoned professional who I'm sure had seen many tears shed over many failed marriages.

Why did I feel like such a failure?

After I shared that our marriage was irreconcilable and that I was definitely prepared to divorce Ahmet, he announced that he believed my husband had sent marital money overseas.

"What? No, that's a ridiculous notion," I defended. "He has no reason to do that. We don't live 'large' but we live comfortably."

Then I let my mind wander where it didn't want to go…

Ahmet is from a male-dominated culture which believes the husband has the ultimate say in a marriage...all decisions, finances, everything...he repeatedly does things without your knowledge...he lies when confronted...the checkbook is a mess with gaps missing—he throws away the bank statements even after you've repeatedly asked to see them...he doesn't do anything unless it benefits himself.

Shit.

Then Adam said something that really shocked me. Since we'd been married for nearly 15 years he felt it leaned in the direction of a long-term marriage. He believed he could get me full ownership of the house— our only tangible asset (at least known to me at the time).

I am still in awe at how Adam evaluated my situation so quickly.

Our Florida residence had been our home for the last 10 years. The home itself was the perfect size for our growing family and it was in a nice neighborhood near some great-rated schools. It certainly wasn't top-of-the-line or pretentious, but it had a fenced yard, a pool, and some other lovely features.

I recalled the day we moved in. Nikole was just shy of 16 months while I was 7 months pregnant with Tarik, although we didn't know he was a "he" at the time. Finding out the sex of our baby before birth was a mistake I wasn't willing to repeat.

You see, when Ahmet learned from the sonogram that our first child was a girl he was, quite frankly, a huge jerk about it for a day or so. He was angry and said all sorts of uncanny things like, "I sent both up there [sperm]...you picked the girl!" and "Damn you, you should have eaten more meat!"

Go ahead, it's ok to laugh. Some of the things he said were funny, in an exasperating way.

He eventually told me he was sorry and that he was happy our baby girl was healthy.

I can't recall many happy memories with Ahmet, but moving in to our new home was one of them for me. After searching several months, I had located this brand-new, four-bedroom, split floor plan all on my own. Of course, he was the negotiator and got us a sensible deal. His job was going outstandingly well and we seemed to be moving up in the world as this was a definite notch (or two) above our previous dwelling. For me, it had held the promise of a new start, a new beginning that was also being marked by the birth of another precious baby.

Ten years later, while we still had a home mortgage to pay off, we also had equity.

Thank God.

This was quite an accomplishment for 2008 since many people were in debt over their heads.

While I was still rejecting the notion that he had been diverting funds overseas, I was quite taken aback by asking for full ownership of the house. I believe my first words to Adam were, "Oh, I couldn't do that. He loves his house."

This is where a good lawyer is so very important because although I was the one filing for divorce, I was clearly too emotional to think of myself and my children's best interests—and there was simply too much at stake.

Here I am ready to leave the father of my children for reasons no one would argue against and I respond, "He loves his house."

He.

Loves.

His.

House?

Chapter Fifteen

Friend, Foe, and the Fool

Although my first inclination was to dismiss what Adam suggested, he had certainly given me something to think about on the drive home. I just wanted to end my marriage, I wasn't looking to be "greedy" and have the house to myself.

Penny was curious as to what was said during my meeting with Adam.

Wow, she's really attentive and concerned...

She thought I should "go for it" like she was doing in her situation. I stated that I wasn't sure I was comfortable going for the full house. She mentioned ever so casually what a smart man Ahmet was; that he seemed to have a good understanding of how to invest money for retirement.

"But he doesn't even have a 401k," I said.

Penny's eyebrows rose ever-so-slightly and her mouth crinkled a tad which encouraged me to press on further.

"Do you know something? Has he ever shared about our finances during one of your talks?" I asked her.

While I was hoping Penny would divulge something to me, I really wasn't expecting her to. Truth is that although she and I were friendly with each other, she was basically just my ride since I was feeling weak and needed someone to be there for me.

I used to get jealous of the times Ahmet and Penny frequently spent together on our outside porch. More than once I had questioned my husband at how comfortable they were with one another—as if they shared more than just cigarettes, alcohol, and laughs.

He assured me that they were just drinking buddies.

And he always told me the truth, right?

Even our kids joked that Penny was Dad's girlfriend and that wasn't funny, I know. At some point I gave up questioning their relationship—I just didn't care anymore.

Although both parties deny any wrong doing, to this day, I don't buy it.

Maybe if she had spent more time with her husband than mine her marriage would have worked out...

I stared at her dead on and finally Penny, no longer perky, back-peddled her statement and said that Ahmet had talked about how "He had retirement covered."

Great, what did that mean?

Chapter Sixteen

Keep Moving Forward

Question:
When you're backed in a corner what do you do?

Answer:
Prepare yourself for battle.

It was five extremely long days after I said I wanted a divorce and Ahmet and I were still living under the same roof. I was trying my best to keep quiet and out of his way. He moved himself into the spare bedroom and we told the kids Daddy was sleeping there because of his back, and for the time being they bought it.

I was actually pretty calm for someone about to divorce after 15 years of marriage. I think it was because I knew it was the right decision. But my acceptance, politeness, and matter-of-factness seemed to be royally pissing Ahmet off more than usual. Maybe I was being too kind.

Is that a thing?

My mom certainly thought I was being too nice given some of the crap my husband had put me through over the years. She didn't even know all of it…

Ahmet started drinking as if alcohol would soon be banned and he would rant and carry on about random things. I strived to keep our conversations to the evenings when our son and daughter were in bed but he wanted to vent when it suited him.

No big surprise there but I didn't want our children to see our mess. I felt we owed it to Nikole and Tarik to try to hold it together and maintain normalcy as much as possible.

I was alone in that line of thinking.

Ahmet, ever the good salesman and strategist, could read me so very well. He always could. He seemed a step or two ahead of me; anticipating my thoughts and actions. At times it felt like he had the house bugged; he knew of conversations when it was just the kids and I in the house.

A lot of his coworkers were divorced and provided their opinion on next moves.

I didn't have any moves!

I wish I did. They could have come in handy.

My only move was to keep moving forward. To end this charade where I needed permission to go have a lunch with any of the few friends I was allowed to have. To do anything for myself that took me out of the house. I could almost see freedom from these chains I was carrying and I desperately wanted to touch the torch of Lady Liberty.

But Ahmet had moves and he wasted no time in going on the offensive. I remember the smugness when he told me he had found and read my personal journal that I kept hidden. It actually wasn't hidden; it was kept in my nightstand. I didn't think I needed to hide it. Inside those pages were my private thoughts. I would gush about my children and share how they were my reason for living and how they had given my life purpose.

There were also many penned pages documenting many a miserable marital episode but Ahmet honed in on the one thing I left vague—whether or not I had cheated on him. For the record, I had cheated on him many times—in my head. In the physical sense, no, never.

Could he dare say the same?

With the tension mounting between us it was no longer possible to hide it from the kids. I had tried to play it by the book as best I could, reading and following the advice of child psychologists and such as to how to tell them. We sat them down to tell them together and they were naturally upset since their whole world was utterly turned upside down. We both tried to reassure them that we loved them, this was their home, and they were safe.

But were they? Was I?

You could tell by the rage in Ahmet's face that he was very angry that I was the one ending this marriage—me, little insignificant me who would be nothing if it weren't for him.

"You would be with some piece of shit American loser in some piece of shit place with some crappy job!" he bellowed. "You were nothing when I found you and I'll make sure you'll have nothing!"

Wow, that's a loving thing to say to the mother of your children.

Chapter Seventeen

God Bless the Cowboy Boot

Question:
What spurs the 'fight' instead of the 'flight'?
Answer:
When you realize you have nothing to lose.

On Tuesday morning with the kids off to school and no job to go to *(I did mention I was career-less and chose this time to leave him, right?)*, I had a lot of time to privately go into hysterics.

Actually, a lot of it was well-founded. His threats just weren't sitting well. He was so angry, not at the thought of our marriage being over, but at the notion that I was the one asking for a divorce.

"How dare she? Who the hell is she? What are people going to think?"

It was his narcissistic tendencies that had me worried. Well that, coupled with his drinking, culture, and religion—all the right ingredients to ignite if threatened. He was becoming unhinged. His charm was no longer working on me. His core was being threatened and there was no telling what he was capable of doing.

I talked with my mom that morning and shared that I was afraid of what he would do. She had never trusted Ahmet. I'm not sure if it was a slight predisposition to his culture or religion, but she'd always been leery of him. Bless her acute maternal instincts. I don't remember what the trigger was but we both got freaked out thinking of worst-case scenarios of what he would do if he continued down this destructive path.

Scenario One: Ahmet explodes and kills me to get me out of the picture.

Scenario Two: He kills our children.

Scenario Three: He takes us all down in a mass-suicide attempt.

Any of those scenarios would be absolutely horrible and it chilled my bones just thinking that way. While a case could be made against being paranoid and prone to watching too many action-thriller movies, my mom asked if Ahmet still owned a gun.

"He said he got rid of it," I told her.

Yet we both knew how he'd lied before.

Crap...does he still own that gun?

I hung up with a promise to her that I'd snoop around to check.

Something made me go straight to his closet in our bedroom.

Do you believe in divine guidance? Gut feelings? Your sixth sense? Pure luck?

I like to define it as that feeling or instinct that culminates in an "ah-ha" moment. I've experienced this more than once in my life, especially while living this nightmare I was caught up in.

Granted, my husband was not a huge collector of things. He came to America with one suitcase and most of what he did have he kept private and his "stuff" was generally contained to three places: his night table, closet, and the garage. So in essence, it's not like I would have had to search the house for hours.

But I really needed to see if he had repurchased a gun or if he had kept the one I insisted he sell when our daughter was born. I did not want a gun in the house for fear of how easy it would be for him to grab when angry; which was far too frequently.

I was drawn to search his suits and found some interesting items in his jacket pockets. Five hundred dollars in cash.

What a dumbass I was not to pocket that money right then.

I also found some interesting blue diamond-shape pills.

Ah, so that's what Viagra looks like...wow, those sure as heck have never been used with me...

Then I glanced down to his boots. His size thirteen shoes could easily conceal a gun. I cautiously reached down and instantly felt something there but it was not at all what I expected.

It was papers, a two-inch wad of rolled up papers.

What on earth?

I removed the rubber band that held it all together and began to unroll...drumroll...our tax returns from the last two years.

Why the hell are these in his shoes?

Then I started to scan some of the numbers, even though I hate numbers.

My Dad's the accountant and all-around good numbers guy. If you try to put numbers in front of me I sort of drift off into another time zone for a bit. I'm a "words" girl. But I wasn't drifting now.

And, if I was reading it correctly, my career-conscientious husband had made more than *TRIPLE* what I thought he did last year; and the year before that!

Well, well, well...this led to a very interesting question...

Where on earth was all this money, since it surely wasn't in our joint bank account?

And just like that, WHAMMO! Another layer of our marriage disintegrated as a new level of deception was unveiled.

Chapter Eighteen

Oh Yeah, Game On Mister!

Question:
Can you say financial infidelity?
Answer:
I can.

To think I actually felt guilty at first that I was calling it quits on my marriage!

My lawyer was ecstatic like it was the eighth day of Hanukah when I presented him with copies of what I had found out. I thankfully did not find a gun during my snooping expedition, but it had been a productive find for sure; not what I had expected, and this was just the beginning of unexpected things to come.

Adam quickly concluded that about one-third of Ahmet's paycheck was being diverted into another bank account.

Where was the money going?

We only had one joint account that I knew of.

I never thought to look into our bank account to see what he was doing with our money because I believed we were a team, building a future *together* with *our* money.

That shit!

I had given him everything—my love, my loyalty, my youth, and in addition to sacrificing my career to cater to him and our children, I had never once, ever, thought about keeping anything just for myself.

Wow.

Adam said what Ahmet had done was "sequester marital funds" and we now had some leverage which would be helpful to present to a judge.

The anger swelled in me like I had just eaten a pound of humus and pita bread. I was fuming as I relived Ahmet's recent words of intimidation to me:

"We split the house 50-50!"

"Don't hire a lawyer or you'll be sorry!"

Oh I was sorry all right.

Sorry I had ever stayed married to this lying, manipulative, sorry excuse of a man.

"I want to go for the house, Adam. Hell yeah, I want the house!" I said.

Chapter Nineteen

The Financial Mistress

Did you know that financial infidelity has a lot in common with the actual act of having a physical affair? Being financially unfaithful requires skills such as lying, cheating, manipulation, and deception.

And I had caught my husband cheating on me *BIG* time!

Turns out Ahmet had been courting his financial mistress for years. I imagine it had been pretty much since the beginning of our marriage.

Adam and I easily found $250 thousand—and that was just on the surface of the previous two years. Imagine if we had dug deeper? Man oh man; I was sure growing up fast after this latest discovery of his infidelity.

How dare he?

I was really outraged and shocked that he felt he needed to keep money from me. I was a very down-to-earth woman who was quite happy with simple things in life. I was never the "high maintenance" pampering type who needed to have her hair, nails, and face continually done (not that there's anything wrong with that at all). And since I never liked my body enough, I almost never wanted to go clothes shopping, so forget being hungry for labels and designer items.

I also didn't require expensive furniture since we were rather rough on it to begin with plus we had young ones. Couple all this with the fact that although I didn't inherit my dad's love of numbers, I did, in fact, inherit his frugal gene—I was, and am, a coupon, deal, and bargain-hunter.

You get the picture.

Why would he not share that he was making a great salary? I would have been proud of him.

Just the year before Ahmet told me we could either get a new bedroom set or I could have Lasik eye surgery—but not both. Guess which one I picked?

If you guessed that I picked the one that both of us could benefit from and enjoy you are correct.

Yet I now find out that we had always been doing quite well for ourselves financially.

Why on earth would he not think whatever he earned, we earned?

Oh, I forgot. It's all about him and what he wants out of life.

With this new realization that Ahmet had been secretly diverting marital funds I thought he would agree that I should get the house outright and the kids and I could stay. My lawyer and I also felt it would be fair to split half of what I had uncovered, which we knew was just the beginning of his nest egg he had squirreled up for himself.

But Ahmet came to our first mediation denying any other bank account existed.

Oh boy. This is going to be a long trip.

Half of what he diverted from our joint bank account was my money, too, by law (and common decency). But legally I would have to swim into Turkish waters and spend money translating to find what was well-hidden oceans away. So fine, I'll settle for being awarded the house.

The once eager, wide-eyed young girl who mutated into a lifeless wife afraid to form her own opinion was done caving in to his demands.

Enter his hot-shot lawyer. Mr. "I'm-so-great-bow-to-me-I-represent-millionaires-who-stick-it-to-their-wives" and charges $400 an hour.

Nice.

And the clincher—his lawyer became a major player for the defense on a high-profile Orlando case, defending a young woman accused of killing her three-year-old daughter.

Fun.

Did I fully know what I was getting myself and the kids into back then? That would be a huge "no." But there's something to be said about having nothing to lose.

I was in that position...about to turn 40, two kids, no job, no savings, no 401k, no kidding.

God, when and how did I get so pitiful?

Chapter Twenty

Spies or More Lies?

When I was in third grade I played *Charlie's Angels* with my girlfriend from my Long Island neighborhood, Massapequa. We'd each pick a lead character to impersonate and make up a crazy scenario that was most likely a combination of several recently-aired episodes, and of course, vow to solve the mystery.

Kris Munroe played by Cheryl Ladd, was my favorite heroine to play.

I guess even though I was in elementary school I bought into that saying that blonds "have more fun." Being a "big-boned" average height brunette, I jumped at the chance to play the stunning blue-eyed blond every time.

"Kris, lookout...he has a gun!" yelled Kelly, played by 9-year-old Tracy.

Tracy was my best buddy ever since we were four. I met her after biting her older brother on the arm. The story goes that little Johnny was just innocently riding his tricycle down our street and I ran over and chomped on his arm for no reason.

What can I say? I was hungry. I'd like to think now that I attacked him because I was actually an intuitively bright child and knew there was something dark about him. I learned he turned to cocaine in his teens, lied and stole from his family, and ended up going to jail after hurting someone pretty badly.

Johnny never played with us. I guess I can't blame him after our abrupt and less than pleasant introduction. But Tracy and I became inseparable and spent hours and days on end together. Her skin was a gorgeous golden color, her legs long and lean and endless. All before puberty—no fair!

I was already jealous of her height and those athletic legs, since it meant she could easily outswim me and glide to the finish line assuring she'd take first- or second-place at our swim meets. I would inevitably place third (which was still awesome, I realize now).

Before Internet and iPhones, we'd play outside on the weekends for as long as we could. We'd create crazy scenarios and take turns spewing cheesy lines similar to the show while acting out dramatic scenes that always seemed to include spying, chasing, and shooting. The lightning bugs would come out and it was our signal to go in since their meek little flashes didn't offer enough light to play.

Ah, those were the creative and carefree days of youth.

Flash forward 33 years later.

It's one thing when it's pretend on television and in the movies—it's a whole other level when reality is involved. Being threatened, chased, and spied on isn't any fun when it's real.

One Wednesday night after taking the kids out for a quick bite to eat, Ahmet declared to me that he had hired a private investigator to "tail me."

I was dumbfounded.

Why on earth did I need tailing? Where did he

think I was going?

"Tail me for what?"

In his chauvinistic and narcissistic infinite wisdom, Ahmet was still convinced that I was having an affair—that it had to be the reason I wanted a divorce. Because why on earth would I ever want to divorce him unless it was for another man?

This bothered him no end and he was intent on finding out my "mystery man." Whenever he spent time with the kids he would interrogate them for most of their time together.

"Who is your mother seeing? What is she doing now? Who comes over to the house?"

Now, I don't know if he actually hired anyone to have me followed. He claims he did and who knows. His judgement has always been clouded by his pride. I do know that if he did hire anyone that it was an absolute waste of good money. Money the kids and I could have put to better use.

"There's no one else and I have never, ever cheated on you," I reiterated. "Man, it must really suck to know that I'm leaving you because of you and not for someone else."

Not my finest fruit-of-the-spirit moment, I know. But it felt good at the time.

Whoa. Hot button.

I proceeded to tell him that if what he said was true, that I'm sure his private investigator was freaking BORED OUT OF HIS MIND! At that time my life consisted of driving the kids to elementary and middle school, both of which were within a three-mile radius.

I'd grocery shop, walk our dog, go to church, and on occasion, head over to the YMCA.

Woohoo...was I living the dream, or what?

I was no saint by any means.

But this was my daily routine: homework and hugs; crying and cooking; waking and walking; repeat.

I was never the partying type but now I most certainly did not have the means or desire or funds to go out. What I was trying to do was salvage my soul and put up a good front for our children that we would all be alright no matter what.

I think Ahmet was starting to do the math and calculate that he had a lot more to lose than just his wife of 15 years.

Chapter Twenty-One

Penny for Your Thoughts

As I mentioned earlier, my next-door neighbor Penny had been the one to drive me to meet my lawyer. Evidently, Ahmet had known about it all along.

I thought I had kept that a secret.

I found this interesting because we met at a local convenience store near the expressway so I could park my car and hop into hers.

Shortly after I hired my bulldog lawyer, a curious development occurred. Ahmet was insane with rage at Penny. He ranted and screamed that he "would bring *her* down!"

Wait…did I hear that right…her?

He then proceeded to say he would make a flyer and tell the whole neighborhood "what a whore" she was.

What…so now he's more pissed at her than me?

Wow, so the fact that she was the one to bring me to the lawyer really must have riled him.

Why? Did she know where the bodies were buried? Wait…the picture's coming into focus now…

Penny was a tremendous flirt who liked to party. It didn't matter to her if a man (or woman I've been told) was married or single. She was a tigress. (She may have a sex addiction.)

One afternoon before the kids were home she bragged that she was "great at sex" and often "had an itch that needed scratching."

Who says that—aside from the fictional character Samantha Jones from "Sex and the City?"

I had always suspected there was more to her relationship with Ahmet. Something had definitely been different between them lately, although I couldn't put my finger on it. Now he was ready to blow a blood vessel as he threatened to "take her down."

Ahmet said he called Penny's soon-to-be ex-husband and gave him quite an earful—a gesture of "bro helping bro."

I'm sure he left out any incriminating details, like how he and Penny were alone several afternoons and how her teenage daughter intercepted a text meant for her mom that read "where should we have sex?" Her daughter had recently confided in Nikole that her mom was getting it on (replace with more colorful teen lingo) with a married man."

Think of Penny what you will, but she did not cower at his threats of public shaming, nor was she in the least bit intimidated by Ahmet's rage. Quite the opposite—she called the police and filed an injunction on him for making verbal accusations a little too loudly. She said she wasn't going to succumb to his slander.

Good for her, I suppose.

To this day, neither of them admitted any wrong doing—well not to me, but something inappropriate happened—or was attempted. If not, why on earth would there be such sustained rage on both parts?

Penny could afford the boldness to rage back. I had our children to think of and console. And we three had to interact with him since he had a legal right to see his children.

Chapter Twenty-Two

Dial 1-800-HITMAN

Question:
How can you tell if a threat is real?
Answer:
Real or not, be ready.

By definition, a threat is a declaration of intent to cause harm or pain.

Ahmet had begun to make some very alarming statements to me about my own well-being and how I should also "watch out." He was not in his right mind when speaking at times and did not seem to be bothered if our poor children had a front row seat to witness it all.

Does he think these outbursts make them empathetic to him?

If that was his line of thinking, it backfired. In just a short span of time, Nikole and Tarik witnessed their father ridiculously drunk "losing it" on not one, but three separate incidences.

We had to lock ourselves away from him twice—once in the bathroom until he passed out. The other, just after he grabbed me by the t-shirt collar and shook me back and forth while he grabbed my wallet and took away my credit card.

But as I said before, he never actually hit me— yet he came damn close that night. So close that the kids came flying out of their rooms at the commotion and were crying hysterically at seeing him almost attack me. He left the room and the kids and I hunkered down for a "sleepover" in mommy's room.

I guess the cat was out of the bag. Dad's "hurt back" wasn't the reason why he was sleeping in the guest bedroom.

Ahmet left for work in the morning and put a note on the fridge that he would move out the next day. I think he scared himself by how close he was to hitting me but I didn't want to take any chances. Whatever. I packed us up to go stay with my parent's until then. The kids were now terrified of him hurting their mom.

After he got what he wanted from the house and our lawyers were made aware, I had the locks changed. I put in padlocks for the backyard after the night he became outraged when he couldn't reach the kids by phone (they were at sleepovers and I was out with a girlfriend). He said he was in our backyard with a gun, patrolling.

Soon after that I offered to watch my friend's dog for him—a nice big, loyal, 90-pound barking yellow Labrador.

Within another month, enter the "hitman" threat.

You would think it should be me to want to hire one, right?

Guess again.

I'll never forget the text I received from Ahmet one Thursday:

"Just in case you need to know, first you, then your mom, then friend 'a', friend 'b', friend 'c' taken care of by me. The rest is already sub contracted by my uncles with no limitations as you know. God bless you."

God bless you?

Oh my God!

I knew full well Ahmet had an uncle or two in Turkey that were associated with the Turkish mafia. This threat had some merit to it.

The kids were in the living room playing on the Wii and I didn't want them to see me wigging out, so I went outside to absorb this new zinger.

In retrospect, going outside in the open was kind of a stupid move, I know.

But that's when I encountered a new layer to the crazy that was unfolding. In just a few moments I see Ahmet's friend, Mustafa, drive slowly by our house. He was with his girlfriend, but I know he has no business in our neighborhood other than to spy on us to do his friend's bidding.

Shit, he has his friends watching me now too…

It made his threat all the more ominous.

Sufficiently shaken, I grabbed the kids and headed over to my friend's home where, at her urging, I spoke with a deputy about filing a domestic violence injunction.

Back to the original question…how can you tell if a threat is real?

It seems this is a gray area especially if no physical harm has come to you. The male officer who took my statement was wonderful and encouraged me to go forward to get an injunction. He said that Ahmet grabbing me was battery and unwilling contact and he thought I had enough cause to prove I needed a restraining order.

The County Courthouse website says: "You may file a Domestic Violence Injunction if you are a victim of domestic violence or have a *reason to believe* you will *become* a victim of domestic violence."

My lawyer was convinced Ahmet was just a bully backed in a corner and that no real harm would come to me. He said it was up to me but that it could also infuriate him further. Still, I felt I needed to let Ahmet know that his behavior toward me was not okay. I went to the court house to file—but the lady there told me most likely my petition would be rejected. In the end, I did not file, but kept careful track and logged all his outbursts.

Sigh.

Sorry kids.

We're in for a very bumpy ride after all.

Chapter Twenty-Three

But, Judge, I Can Explain

At the time Ahmet moved out, he left $2,000 in our joint checking account. Our mortgage was $1,800 a month and I had an expensive leased car in my name that got a whopping 13 miles to a gallon for $450 a month. There was no 401k, although he'd made six figures for the last 13 years.

Nice.

Oh, did I mention that I did not even have a bank account of my own when I was laid off from the school where I worked?

Double nice.

So, here I was unemployed, financially screwed, and nearly 40 years old.

Talk about failing every question on the "rank-your-stress-level" quiz!

For a while, it was actually all right. I got reacquainted with maintaining a checkbook again (something I had been denied access to many years ago). I was more than capable of balancing a checkbook, mind you, but Ahmet belittled me and said that I "always screwed things up." We were late on a credit card bill *once*.

Um, forgive me. I just gave birth to our second child and have two babies just 18 months apart!

Now I realize that this was just his tactic and shrewd way of keeping me in the dark about how the money—and just how much—was being distributed among *his* bank accounts.

At the temporary hearing held a few weeks after I filed for divorce I was awarded a very fair child support allotment and could comfortably maintain the bills and our lifestyle. I freely admit that comforting our children through this transition was my number one priority—looking for work was second. And with the amount I initially received I could manage to pay our bills, as well as keep the pool and lawn services going; which in turn, kept these individuals whom we had employed for years, working as well.

All this dramatically changed however, when Ahmet realized that this "temporary" (as he believed) predicament wasn't temporary. We were, in fact, headed for a divorce as I found the footing toward freedom and was walking through that door no matter how hard it was.

The more I stood on my own, the more he abhorred me. He told someone we both knew that he didn't like that I was so "together" and that my life was continuing without him, but he would fix that.

With a simple refiling of financial statements and a call to his hot-shot lawyer, we were back in court in a few months. This time to reduce the amount he paid in child support because "the recession had affected his business."

While I don't deny that 2008 was the beginning of a hard-hitting recession in the U.S., in all the years I had known Ahmet, he was now living larger than ever before. Spending money like he was an Arabian prince, excuse me, Turkish prince, with no regard for consequences.

For starters, he moved into an upscale apartment downtown (the penthouse) and in record time, completely equipped his swank digs with new furniture (since he didn't want any of our "old stuff"). The luxury apartment was only a one-bedroom suite because, you know, why should his son or daughter have their own bed (or room) when they stay over?

Um, Mr. Judge…if he's hurting financially, why does he also have a whole new designer label wardrobe?

Top-of-the line new cell phone?

And a new 42" Blu-ray flat screen?

Because he doesn't want any of our old crap!

Yet, here he was now trying to tell the judge we had very expensive furniture he was leaving behind. Another financial anomaly was that although he had never bought Nikole or Tarik gifts before, he had no problem now spending money on them.

And he spent *lots* of money on them including a PS3 and Xbox game system to accompany the newly bought 51" flat screen for our son; Apple iPad; Prada sneakers; VIP tickets to concerts and sports games; annual waterpark passes; and regularly doled out $100 bills to each of them when they saw him. Oh, my favorite: he paid for an NBA mascot to make a special house delivery on Valentine's Day bearing big gifts for our kids.

But Ahmet produced financial documents from his work (which I believe to be doctored) that showed he was making less money—way less money—like less than what he had made 10 years ago. He told the judge he was poor and in debt.

Your honor, this debt occurred after we split and if he was truly making the amount he says he is he would never stay in this country...

Sadly, Mr. Judge sided with Ahmet, and falsified or not, child support and alimony was reduced to one-third of the original amount.

Madness.

Now we're in trouble.

Ahmet was cockier than ever after that and muttered to me as I was exiting chambers that he was "Sorry this hearing did not go in your favor. You know I've hidden the money so well that you and your lawyer will never find it. You're getting nothing."

Then he had the balls to say that I should tell my lawyer to get a new suit, "but he's not done shitting on it yet."

So, in addition to sequestering money away, he was still making at least 10k a month but made it look like a fraction of that.

Now there's justice for you.

Chapter Twenty-Four

Food Angels

Question:
When is it ok to accept help?
Answer:
Any time it is offered.

On an ultra-tight budget, it wasn't long before I realized that even my food shopping regime was about to drastically change. Gone were the days of putting anything the kids or I wanted in the grocery cart. I had never concerned myself with staying within a budget because, well thankfully, I never really had to since college.

If you can relate to that last sentence, let me congratulate you. You are what I consider "budget blessed." I know not everyone will be able to relate to this part of my story but as part of my budget education I quickly realized that brand loyalty was for royalty.

Exaggerating a tad here, but in our case, my affection for certain labels went out the window on most of our beloved items.

Generic items were generally acceptable, and I found creativity in presenting them to Nikole and Tarik as they started questioning our financial stability.

Did you know often times people, especially children, are none the wiser if you sneak the generic brand into the old familiar packaging?

87

This works particularly well on most cereals, condiments, and crackers. Yup, I sneaked for a bit.

You really can't blame me for trying. The kids and I went from dining at nice steakhouses to couponing and bargain buy-one-get-one meals. I got reintroduced to Chef Hamburger helper-like meals and Ramen noodles; which the kids thought was yummy.

Buying soda ranked almost equally to ordering Dom Pérignon.

We ate fine, don't get me wrong. My parents, bless their hearts, would buy extra meat and say that they bought too much and fill our freezer. Or take us out to eat somewhere nice.

This tight-budget experience was really eye-opening, and I quickly noticed that fruits and veggies never appear as BOGO (buy one, get one free) items, nor are they couponed.

Why is it that money goes a lot farther when you buy filling-but-bad-for-you meals?

High-calorie, high-fat, and high-sodium meals are often cheap, discounted, and sold in bulk.

And people wonder why our country has health issues, such as obesity and diabetes?

Sadly, this is the time when the kids and I proceeded to pack on plenty of pounds. Well, this plus emotional and stress eating.

I'll never forget two of my most humbling experiences during this financially dark time. First, I qualified for the reduced lunch rate that offered my children a meal while in school.

Never did I think I would need this, but given

our situation, and the fact that I had no means of fully supporting myself just yet, I took the assistance when the form came home from school. I could not hide this from our kids, nor could I camouflage it differently since the forms had to be turned in to their teachers.

It was heartbreaking to see the concern on my kids' faces for fear that their teachers and friends would look at them differently. They didn't (or not that I was told). I had new appreciation for our school system and this newly single mom appreciated the extra assistance.

The second experience came when I noticed discounted foods could be purchased monthly through a local church ministry. I could fill out the form online then go pick it up at the church.

I won't soon forget that horribly humid July day that I set out to pick up our select groceries. I told the kids I had an errand to run that morning since I didn't want them to come or stress them out more. As it was, they were far too aware of mommy's budget constraints—and new obsession over spending. I sat in my car at the church parking lot for a good seven minutes since my legs felt weighted down by my failed marriage. I didn't want to get out. I felt exposed, vulnerable...

What if someone recognizes me?

I was embarrassed, sad, and…angry.

So angry!

Ahmet was living in a prestigious penthouse, blowing up his credit cards without a care in the world while I was struggling to stay afloat, keep sane for our kids while I restarted my life.

On the flip side, I was also thankful. Thankful that this was a simple way for me to supplement our food supply and it wasn't our only means of sustenance. We had a nice home to live in (although the mortgage payment ate most of what I received from Ahmet). We were not homeless and living on the streets, unsure of where our next meal would come from.

I got choked up when I received the food. I wanted to thank them, to let them know how this helped me out, but so many emotions flooded me. Back in the safety of my car, I cried.

So this is what it's come to...resorting to discounted meals while my ex is living large...

What have I done?

Chapter Twenty-Five

Destination Divorce - Roadblock Ahead

While both kids had the blissful distraction of school (I'm sure they'd love to argue that "blissful" and "school" should never be used in the same context), I had no job to go to, and no energy to do much more than slump hard into depression.

Well, maybe not "hard." And I'm not so sure I slumped. It was actually kind of a gradual slouching. At least it seemed that way to me at the time but my own lens was far from objective.

I felt exhausted from treading water and yet I knew I was nowhere near the shoreline, but I had to keep looking up to the sky in order to breathe. More often than not, the waves seemed to be winning. I continued to bob along and just roll with it.

I thought I was putting up a pretty good front of being "together." After all, I was functioning.

I got up in the morning.

Fed the kids.

Showered.

Got dressed.

Got them off to two different schools.

Not always in that order, mind you, but I was functional.

Most days.

Ah, life had definitely become less joyful and I really felt zapped of energy most of the time.

There's a saying that if you want something done you should give it to the busiest person because you know he/she will make the time to get it done.

I was like that once—a busy woman juggling life.

That was pre-split of course.

I wasn't Superwoman by any means although I did dress the part one Halloween. It was a homespun costume too—red cape, blue sweatpants, white shirt with a big ole felt 'S' triangle cut out and pinned to it. I was so proud of my pre-Pinterest creation.

But other than getting the kids off to school in a timely matter, I had nothing to fill my time. Nothing to do except to reflect on how bad things had become. I talked with my mother sometimes several times a day. I think her maternal instinct kicked in high gear and she knew she should keep a close eye on me and offer support.

For a while I think I was actually waiting for my life to magically, miraculously come together—if I could just get to the finish line of our divorce being finalized.

Limbo is a hard place to be. It's not life-threatening illness or homelessness hard, mind you, but everything about my world seemed to be a big question mark and on hold.

Would I be awarded the house and maintain a place to live?

Would I be able to afford to keep it on my own?

How much child support per month could I count on?

What kind of job can I get where I haven't worked in a while?

When will I find one?

Not knowing how much I had angered the archangel and not knowing what he would try next was working out in Ahmet's favor.

I thought that once I had purchased my one-way ticket to Destination Divorce, I would be travelling via superhighway. But in my case, far from taking the freeway, I got stuck in gridlock early on.

It would take me three years to cross that damn finish line!

Yes, you read that right.

My journey took *THREE* long years before my divorce was finalized.

The courts were backed up, lawyers have their own schedule, and judges are on a rotation basis and can issue new stipulations before they'll hear you. The odds of ending our marriage in a timely fashion were not in our favor.

And the timing was just as it should have been.

Crazy statement to make but there was a reason for our painstakingly slow divorce process and I can tell you in less than 15 words...

God knew I needed time to get myself strong, to mentally steel myself for battle.

My ultimate victory would not be what a judge decided my future should be, but how I would be able to stand on my own two feet when it was all over.

Chapter Twenty-Six

Net Worth

I know Ahmet's murky heart believed I was intentionally not getting a job, so I could be awarded alimony. I'll admit I felt I most certainly deserved it. What I couldn't admit at the time, was that I had lost nearly all my self-esteem and was suffering from depression. I felt his lawyer would love to use that nugget against me.

Trying to find work in my former field was proving difficult since there just wasn't anything to be found nearby that matched. Through another mom at school, I was finally able to secure a part-time, work-from-home job which was perfect for providing some income on my own. It wasn't really what I wanted to do and the hours per week were not consistent, but it was income nonetheless.

I was actually getting crafty at learning how to sustain myself without a full-time job—all without resorting to doing anything illegal, thank you. I scraped together what I could. Sold some old furniture and nick knacks I could easily part with. I saw a flyer advertising a "We Buy Gold" fundraiser being held for a non-profit I knew so I decided to cash in on some of my precious gold jewelry I had been given when I married my Turkish "prince." It now felt like these beautiful 18-carat-shiny gold trinkets were some sort of marital enslavement payment anyway.

A word to the wise: Be careful when selling jewelry or anything that could be viewed as "assets." Lawyers, especially opposing lawyers, love to find this out.

I didn't know, honest!

But it covered July's mortgage and I desperately needed it. Ahmet had warned me that I should cash in my IRA (which could only cover the mortgage for two months) unless I wanted to bounce checks.

I was done with taking financial advice from him!

You've heard of selling the "shirt off your back?" Well I found a place to do that. I sold a multitude of clothes at a plus size consignment shop (nope, I ain't no size two).

Yes, I learned to put pride aside as I learned to survive.

But sinking lower on the financial scale really pulls you down on the emotional scale. I found myself withdrawing deeper and deeper into myself; not reaching out to friends I knew would be there and would willingly give me a lift up. It's so hard to call up someone out of the blue and ask for a listening ear— especially when you think all you'll manage to do is cry.

What a downer!

I knew I could have called and blubbered to a number of people, but our "must do something/be busy" culture makes you feel like you can't just "chill" with others—you have to *do* something when together with friends. Like go out to lunch or coffee, see a movie; something that costs *money* which I did not have to spend.

But I recognized that I needed to get out of the house more and do something for me. I wanted; I needed to start socializing with other adults again—and not just to commiserate with me on what a shmuck my ex was being.

I've never been one to adore waking up early, and I never liked to run. Hell, the only way you'll see me run is if someone is chasing me with a knife or chainsaw. Even then, my first instinct is to turn around, admit defeat, and say, "You got me."

I most certainly did not inherit the running or fitness gene (hence the plus size clothes). But I do love tennis. I have ever since ninth grade when I took it for a PE credit. My dad and I would go and play some weekends at the neighboring Catholic school courts. I will never play Wimbledon but I could hustle and return that spiffy sphere within the lines a good majority of the time.

Like I said, the only official tennis I had played was in high school but I met this remarkable lady at church one morning. Carrie was about 10 years older than I, had five kids, and was in fabulous shape. She was also a competitive tennis player and led a women's cardio tennis group at her house on Tuesday mornings.

Yes, at her house.

She and her husband had a gorgeous home complete with a tennis court at her disposal. She opened her humble abode to share the "love" with women who desired friendship and fitness.

After spending some time talking with me at a

picnic gathering, Carrie encouraged me to come and join them to try it. I think she realized how badly I needed to be among other nurturing women.

I can't describe how good it felt to get back in the swing of things and wield that racket! Sure, I was rusty, and again, far from a pro, but I had some game and was enjoying the productivity of *doing something* and the fact that it was *something for me* was sheer bonus.

Not only was the physical release so refreshingly uplifting, but I was among wonderful women with tremendous compassion. We would laugh at silly maneuvers and would scream and moan as Carrie turned drill sergeant, determined to make sure there wasn't an ounce of us not covered in sweat. The hour would go by so fast that even though I was completely exhausted by the end of it, I didn't want it to end.

I couldn't wait until next week when I could do it all over again.

Then finances got so tight from some unexpected home repairs that crept up: new pool pump, kitchen pipe burst, dryer exploded—nothing major.

While Carrie only charged a mere $6 a class per participant for her cardio tennis session and her professional expertise, I had to face facts that playing tennis was a recreational expense, a luxury if you will. Keeping the electricity on was more of a bona-fide necessity.

Carrie saw how tennis was saving my sanity, as well as helping me slenderize my supersize. She privately told me that I had to keep coming but she didn't want me to pay. As much as I hated the thought of being a "charity case" I hated the thought of not playing tennis or getting to be with these women even more. I accepted her gracious offer to play weekly and to pay only if I felt I could.

A few months later on her birthday, Carrie casually asked if anyone wanted to join her for breakfast after a tennis workout. Everyone enthusiastically agreed to go—everyone except me. I stayed silent.

I smiled and nodded as if to say, "of course I'll be there," but my head was screaming at me, "you don't have the money to go."

We drove in separate cars to our dining destination and the notion to flee and head home floated across my mind.

But this was Carrie. This day was a celebration of her life.

How could I not go?

If this were a cartoon story you could picture the little angel on one side of my shoulder saying: *"Just get water or order cheap toast."*

On the other side was a little devil with a pitchfork, *"You can eat—just charge it—there's room on your credit card."*

Regardless, I listened to the little red guy (or did I?) and went to join my amazing friends. I was so glad I did since I adored our girlfriend gathering and was prepared for better budgeting elsewhere in my week.

The bill came and Carrie surprised us all by saying the meal was on her. Everyone was shocked and argued that it was *her* birthday and no way should she treat us. My eyes instantly welled with tears and I tried to let the seat swallow me up since I just couldn't make them stop (they never do once the first droplets pour out of the gate). Soon everyone noticed and was concerned if I was ok and asking what was wrong.

All I could do was stumble through some words explaining how I almost didn't join them because I didn't have the money to pay for my bill but I didn't want to go home yet and not be with them.

My confession yielded stunned silence.

Seriously, what do you say to that?

Carrie just looked at me with her soft, Hershey-like eyes and softly spoke, "Suzan, thank you. I kept hearing God telling me to pay the bill and you just confirmed that I heard Him. It's the most beautiful birthday gift ever."

The times I had with these eight great women, both on and off the court, are precious to me to this day.

Chapter Twenty-Seven

How Do You Stop This Nightmare?

Worse than our financial situation was the mental anguish Ahmet was heaping on our children on a regular basis. My new friendships couldn't have come at a better time since I would also seek their parental counsel during all this ugliness that was being inflicted on us.

From the start of our separation, Ahmet relied on manipulation, threats, and mind games. Alcohol can make you say and do crazy things and if you take the alcohol away what are you left with? I guess just the crazies. He was prone to rambling tirades and talking in circles that would inevitably end up in threats to engage the lawyers.

That seemed to be where we were at—smack dab in the middle of trying-to-divorce-this-crazy-man-keep-my-kids-safe-while-looking-for-a-job life.

Nikole and Tarik never quite knew which Dad would be picking them up for their visits—would it be the benevolent "Baba" who would buy them anything their tender hearts asked for—or would it be the indifferent, inebriated, angry Dad who would say nasty shit to them and was seeing them because it was "his time" to see them. Or at least that's how they felt.

Regardless of "who" would be arriving, both children developed severe anxiety before each scheduled visit for various reasons. Never mind the times he would ask them if he could "just swing by" and bring them dinner or something. Those unscheduled times really bothered them and would cause a whole new spiral of anticipation.

It wasn't without cause. Our babies were just old enough to understand the horrors of what was happening. Watching their father rage and unravel; watching their mother cry, fret, and withdraw in fear. If Ahmet wanted to kill me, he could. I'd die just once.

If he killed our children, I would die every single day of my life.

That was my biggest fear. Not about not being able to take care of us. Not about ever finding love again. My deepest fear that haunted my waking hours was him hurting me by hurting our children.

Tormenters have been known to snap before. The story of a local sheriff who shot and killed his own two children before killing himself was fresh in my mind. I could only pray that wouldn't happen to us.

Ahmet was shrewd and knew how to manipulate and talk a tremendous game. This served him well as a persuasive salesman, but inflicted hell as a father.

He'd spew calculated sayings that tore into their soul and safety like:

"It's my house. Take care of it. I may be the one living here in a few months."

"Don't worry; you'll be done with me soon."

"I want to take you to Turkey this summer."

"Why don't we just never see each other ... I'll wait a few years for you to grow up!"

Our son believed this threat and worried that his dad would find a new family and he and Nikole would be forgotten. Little did we know then it would become a wish we hoped would come true.

Ahmet told me if I tried to keep his kids away from him, he'd quit his job and they'd foreclose on the house, and he would move back to Turkey.

Good, go, I'll deal...goodbye!

I wanted to shield my babies as much as possible but sometimes with him it was impossible. Like the time after he had moved out of the house but slipped into my room when I was out walking the dogs. Nikole had tried to stop him but he barged in and I caught him exiting with a duffle bag, which I questioned. He was pissed off and cursed me out on our front lawn in front of my friend and her tween son.

"This is why we don't live under the same roof together!" he barked to the kids. Nikole flicked his rum-filled Solo cup out of his hand and said, "No, this is why!"

A few hours later, Ahmet called the kids and said he was sorry. But damage had been done. Seeing him go from fine to indifferent to outraged in less than 10 seconds scared them; couple that with threats to their mom.

They wanted time alone with him like they wanted to go to the dentist.

Ahmet took the kids for Thanksgiving Eve so they would be with me on Thanksgiving. I really didn't want to stay home alone on my rare "kid-free" night, so

I went by myself to go help sort canned food at a local food bank.

I'm not sure what Ahmet said to our daughter, but she called me twice, texted four times, begging to come home within two hours of them being together. She told her dad she didn't want to stay with him and said he first got very mad then sad. When I explained to him that I wasn't currently at home but would be by 9:30 p.m., Ahmet accused them that they were only seeing him because I had a date and he was pissed.

"Your whore mom has plans so you have to stay!" he told them.

Oh, Ahmet, you say such great things to our children.

I shouldn't have been that surprised at the way he talked to them. In my opinion, Ahmet was never good at parenting, even when we lived together. He admitted that he didn't want to discipline them or make hard decisions. They were expected to listen and obey him at all times, but what he really wanted most was to be their friend, their buddy, to be adored.

Sure, show me a child who wants a bully as a buddy.

The kids' anxiety about seeing and spending time with their father increased, the more they wanted to stay with me and back out of the schedule he'd arranged. He saw this as my "masterminding" and "brainwashing" them not to see him. He even got his lawyer involved who warned my lawyer about his client's *parental alienation* crap.

No, judge, he's just being a horrid father!

It was a hard place for all of us to be and for the life of me, I wish I could have made it go away.

Make *him* go away.

Another source of nightmares was how Ahmet was suddenly interested in Tarik and Nikole's academic and extracurricular functions now that we were separated.

Our son was so nervous that his dad was coming to his fifth-grade winter holiday performance because that meant both mom and dad were going to be there. "It'll be fine," I told him. "We both love you and just want to be there for you."

Truth is that if I had claws I would have released them at this time. Ahmet never attended school events. I was always the one, the *only* one, who attended their activities. I was an extremely active parent, from serving as a PTA board member to being a Girl Scout leader, classroom mom, and on one occasion, soccer coach. I lived to be involved in my children's lives almost as much as I loved being their mom.

But for this event, Ahmet insisted he was coming too, which was ironic since he never could take off from work for school events. But now that we were divorcing, he was outraged if I dared try to keep him away.

He showed up at the event and came to sit behind his daughter and me. I can't say for sure if he had been drinking or not, but it turns out our son was right to be nervous about this night.

Somewhere in my impending ex's head was the notion that I must have been screwing all the fifth-grade fathers and that's why I wanted a divorce. Every guy I talked with or who befriended me was a suspect—married men, gay men, it didn't matter.

Damn if only I believed I was that desirable and in demand!

At the end of the performance, Ahmet came over to Jay, the dad of our son's friend, John. Our boys played well together, and his wife, Jenna, was very sweet. Ahmet made it clear that he didn't "care for" or trust Jay, but the kids and I liked spending time with them. For whatever reason, he got right in Jay's face, made an accusation that involved me, then flicked his finger across Jay's chin taunting him to strike.

The night ended with the principal and assistant principal ending the altercation, as they escorted Ahmet outside to cool off. Jay warned him if he tried something like that again, he'd press charges. Our son was mortified, Jenna and I dumbfounded.

I get it, sure—if I were to have an affair it would be with my friend's husband and my son's friend's father, right?
Oh, we're having so much fun now!

Chapter Twenty-Eight

The Son Always Shines

If you asked Ahmet if he loved his children, of course he would say, "Yes." If you asked him to pick his "favorite" or confess to whom he loved more he would pause for good measure but say, "they're both special to me but my son is my namesake."

The Turkish culture, while more modern than many other Middle Eastern countries, is predominantly patriarchal in its philosophy. Males most certainly reigned in Ahmet's family. The sun revolved around Ahmet and his younger brother.

Poor second-born sister Aleyna was ranked "last" even though she was loving and loyal of the bunch to their *anne* (Turkish for mother; pronounced *Ah-nay*). Though Aleyna was college educated and worked full time teaching elementary students, she had little say in her marriage or finances. Her husband was in charge of the family and money and even when he was laid off from work for a spell, Aleyna had to obediently follow his wishes.

I could tell from the beginning that Ahmet would treat our little girl differently too. The disappointment of a daughter being born first may have dulled slightly upon her arrival, but he never fully embraced the beauty or blessing it was to create life. Boy or girl shouldn't matter; it is a precious gift from God.

Even though that sweet little gift, my baby girl, almost killed me...

When you're set to induce, you feel certain your baby will be born that day. Well, my little one had other plans. For the next 26 hours and after numerous bags of Pitocin, delivery wasn't happening. I was discharged and put on bed rest to keep my blood pressure down.

Four days later my water broke while at my doctor's office.

"Good," he said. "I was putting you back in the hospital anyway."

Nearly 20 hours from the point of my water breaking, my kidneys had shut down. I needed an emergency Caesarean.

This completely devastated my parents for my dad's sister had died of kidney failure. Given all the trauma and drama we found ourselves going through, it was Ahmet who complained he was exhausted from sleeping in the chair next to me.

It was as if he didn't hear the part that my life was on the line. He was elated that they were going in to get her to "put an end" to this time zap.

I was awake in the operating room and asked Ahmet if they had cut me yet. His loving reply, "Oh, yes. They had to cut through a lot of fat."

Our little 8-pound 8-ounce tiger arrived with a hearty cry. She was pink and perfect and had a headful of dark hair. (The nurse admitted that she panicked slightly since she wasn't used to having to "work up a lather" when shampooing newborns.) My kidneys and blood pressure, thankfully, returned to normal.

I was in love with Nikole instantly, even after such a difficult birth. She knows my first endearing words to her were, "Why'd you try to kill mommy?"

And each year, four days before her actual birthday, I remind her that we could be celebrating her birthday already had she not been so stubborn.

That first night in the hospital, our little girl cooed and stretched (she finally had room—she was 21.5 inches long) and made the most amazing little baby noises. Ahmet was less than thrilled to have his sleep interrupted yet again. Somewhere in the middle of the night he yelled at her to "shut up."

Too numb for words, I said nothing but thought, "Dear God, I just made him a father."

A year and a half later, our son's birth was a totally different scenario.

After 40 hours of labor (yeah, I know, I can make them and bake them just fine; can't seem to deliver them), Ahmet was present and proud and nearly cried when he saw it was a boy. He gave me a dozen red roses and a 1-carat diamond ring for producing him a son; my reward. At Nikole's birth, I received three red carnations. Oh, and after Tarik was born, Ahmet ordered a lamb be slaughtered and sacrificed in Turkey.

I think you get the picture.

What an incredible blessing to have two healthy and intelligent children! Each of them is unique and special—I could never pick a favorite; I love them equally and unconditionally. They are my two amazing sources of happiness that resulted from my marriage to Ahmet.

Sadly, there are many instances where Nikole was treated less than favorably by her father. Ahmet is a rather narrow-minded, unrelenting man who prides himself on image (you probably get that already); he believes worth is measured not by the size of one's heart, but rather the appearance in the mirror and size of the pocketbook.

I came to know this as our marriage evolved. I knew how he talked about others behind their back. I knew he could be shallow and unforgiving in his views. I just never thought he'd lash out at our young daughter and inflict such deep-rooted pain.

Until Nikole confided in me and shared a letter she wrote to her father when she was 16. These are her words:

"I remember you called me into your room after I had had dessert. You told me I was fat and needed to stop eating. You told me I was a disappointment and that your friend's daughters were skinny so I should be too. I was an embarrassment to you. I couldn't have been older than 9 by then. In the morning, when I was so hurt and felt betrayed, you acted as if everything was normal.

You probably don't remember, but I do. Alcohol may have taken away your memory, but mine was fully intact. This type of incident happened repeatedly while we lived under the same roof, and I felt worthless. I quit the swim team because you told me you were too embarrassed to see me in a swimsuit in front of the other girls. According to you, I was too slow anyway. I would never be good enough.

This set the standard for how I viewed myself

growing up, and it's damaged me immensely. My father, who was supposed to build me up and show me what love is, was the one who took little pieces of me over time. Once at dinner, I was quiet. I didn't really talk at all because that's how I learned to cope—to keep my head down. You got angry and went off on me for being ungrateful. I told you I was just trying to have a calm dinner with you, but you said I was worthless. I went to the bathroom. Tarik said you cursed me out and people were staring. You came into the bathroom, where I had been crying, and told me to get out. When I came back you said you were done with me until I grew up and 'loved and respected you right.' Then you told me you always had more fun with Tarik and that I should stay home from then on."

This is just a sampling of some of the horrific things he'd say and do to his firstborn. Nikole is incredibly beautiful and strong, eloquent and wise beyond her years. She's a fighter. Thank God she has opened up to offload some of the pain and shame she endured at his hands.

Thank God we got out…

He may have been, as my lawyer eloquently nailed it, "a shitty father," but he was still her father, and since he never beat her or put her in real physical danger, the courts demanded regular visitation.

There it is again! Why, as a society, do we feel we have just cause to block someone only from hurting us with their fists?

When you degrade your daughter, you are teaching her to doubt herself, hesitate, hold back true feelings. It may cause her to view verbal insults or physical harm as normal, she may hate herself or start to self-harm.

When you degrade your own daughter, you have damaged someone's sister, future wife, mother, grandmother.

Chapter Twenty-Nine

Say it With Me,
"Therapy is Our Friend"

It was soon apparent that the kids and I needed lots and lots of therapy on a regular basis to help us with what we were going through. Finding a therapist within my budget, of like, zero dollars, wasn't going to be easy. I guess it was fate that I had a wee nervous breakdown on church grounds and we were granted some counseling sessions for free.

Seeing my kids hurting so badly I just didn't want to go home one morning after I dropped them off at school. So I drove around and soon found myself bawling hysterically at our church parking lot. I made my way inside and Pastor Ray promptly escorted me to the on-campus Counseling Center where I was granted four family therapy sessions at no cost.

Thank you, God!

I was truly frightened by Ahmet's irrational state and started questioning his next move:

Is he just full of talk?

Will he make good on his word and physically harm me?

Was he mad enough to actually hurt our children?

These questions, along with other frightening

thoughts, played repeatedly in my head like a record needle stuck in the same scratched groove. In my defense, my line of thinking was not really that far off. Bullies have been known to snap before.

Sadly, there have been several incidents right in Florida and it was not uncommon to hear of husbands going on a rampage and killing their own children to punish the ex-wife. Plus, in addition to alcohol, factor in narcissistic machismo and you had the conditions for a perfect storm.

While a couple of pro-bono therapy sessions granted by the church were deeply appreciated, quite frankly we needed more. It's almost tragic to admit that if my husband had beaten our bodies instead of just battering our souls we would have received more attention and assistance.

When the counseling sessions ran out we seemed caught in limbo for a time. After some guidance from a few friends, we came across some generous counselors that understood our situation and dramatically reduced their rates. Putting a price tag on mental health is so sad. After all, if your mind isn't well you can't function in life. Mental stability was important for sure, but so was keeping a roof over our heads and food in our tummies—that took priority over talking out our problems.

Although I believed in God, I had never considered myself a very religious person up until this point in my life. On occasion during our 15-year marriage (especially when we weren't doing well), I found myself wanting to connect with a spiritual community. But Ahmet would discourage me from attending and I would give in since I didn't want it badly enough and didn't have the strength to battle him over it.

So as trite as this may sound to some, it's during this mess of my life that I found God.

Or rather, He found me.

No, I found Him. He had always been there—waiting.

Now I'm not saying that God is for divorce, but I do solemnly believe that he never intended us to live in fear and be held in spiritual captivity. I found new strength in my total surrender and admission of my sins. It was no mistake that it was at a church parking lot when my decision to leave Ahmet was solidified.

It's poignant how threats to personal safety and facing one's own mortality give way to discussions of heaven and afterlife. When Nikole and Tarik learned they had not been baptized as babies, they decided it was something they both wanted.

The children and I were baptized on August 18, 2010.

We talked about it but, no, their dad was not told of this before the event. It seemed like my eyes were opening for the first time as I reaffirmed my faith.

When I was just a young 20-something, it never bothered me that Ahmet was Muslim. I thought that since both of us, and our religions, believed in God, it would be enough.

It wasn't.

I didn't realize the religious divide between

Jesus and Mohammed was wider than the East is from the West. I envisioned that we could raise our children with the knowledge and teachings of both religions: I could share Biblical concepts and teach about Jesus, and he could read the Quran to them. In some marriages, it has worked.

Just not in ours.

I've always been a rather laid-back kind of girl—quite accepting of different viewpoints, but religion was an all-or-nothing thing for Ahmet, and if he couldn't get his way, by default, it was nothing.

While therapy can do wonders, there's always a cost involved to receive it. Prayer was, and is, free. There's no charge to talk to God and you have an unlimited minutes plan.

No press 1 for English.

No appointment needed.

No elevator-hold music to endure.

No "closed" because it's afterhours.

God is open for therapy 24/7/365.

So, I latched on to the free prayer concept and still do. We have been so fortunate to have so many people praying for us and cheering us on. We needed it too. I felt as if a whole legion of angels were needed for what we were up against.

The painstaking slow court process, coupled with his overall "un-wellness" caused our children a lot of hurt, and the more my children hurt, the more I hurt. Ahmet had always enjoyed dancing with the devil—like grabbing me by the neck collar, stalking our backyard one night with a gun, or saying that he had his uncles arrange a hit on my life.

My lawyer acknowledged his behavior to us sucked and he was sympathetic, but he didn't feel we had enough to legally deny visitation. He did say that while I had to make the kids available to him for his scheduled visits, it was up to Nikole and Tarik whether they would get in the car with him. They were old enough to show resistance.

Sure, it's easy to tell your kids, "You *don't have to go with daddy if you don't want* to..." but so much harder to carry it through. This was their father after all. Someone they were used to seeing at home every day. Someone they loved and wanted approval from.

The angst and torture of weekly visits took their toll, since nearly every time spent with him had some drama to it, for one or both of them. The negative repercussions mounted, and their very safety and security was shaken to its core.

On New Year's Eve Ahmet sat both kids down at 10:30 p.m. and forced them to endure his *divorce talk* until midnight. During that one-and-a-half hour drunken rambling, I was called a "cheating whore" and my mom, their Grandma, was the "biggest bitch in the world." Tarik was told to "stop crying like a baby; boys don't cry" and he yelled at Nikole to "stop being a little bitch like your mother."

When it was finally over, the kids said they locked themselves in the bedroom until morning.

Both kids were having intense and disturbing dreams about their dad. The nightmares usually ended with Ahmet murdering me. Nikole's often included that her dad would kill her too. Our daughter would later be diagnosed and treated for post-traumatic stress disorder.

My God, how do we stop this?

Should I run away?

The thought had occurred to me, but he had more resources to find me than I had to hide somewhere. Plus, what kind of life would it be hiding?

Tarik shared with his counselor that he was so worried about Dad's anger, and that "life was no longer fun" and he wanted to kill himself.

Sweet baby, it will get better...

But I, too, wanted to be swallowed up and taken away from earth as I sobbed on my bedroom floor that night.

I prayed my boldest prayer:

"God, please help. Hear me. My babies can't take any more. I can't take anymore. Please, remove him from our lives. I don't care how. I'm not praying for his death although that's up to you. I can't pray that. But maybe he should return to Turkey to be with his family. He's not happy or healthy. Lord, I don't know how, but please, in your son's name, remove him from our lives..."

The very next night, Sunday at 7:42 p.m., the doorbell rang.

It was someone from the Department of Children and Families.

Chapter Thirty

That Just Happened!

The knock on the door jolted our hearts. I answered cautiously, wondering who the heck it was.

Thank God I'm still dressed!

I saw a lady wearing dress pants and a white blouse through our peephole. I saw her credentials and allowed her inside our home. She said her office had received a call to investigate. Someone had reported that Ahmet had compromised their safety. She wanted to speak privately with Nikole and Tarik. She didn't want to speak with me. I could go about my business.

God, you're here—you came!

This opening of the door brought hope—for the first time in such a long time.

I assured the kids to just share whatever was on their hearts and left the room, so she could talk with both children freely. I went to my bedroom, nearly put a hole in my carpet from all the repetitive pacing and started talking to God.

I had no concern about what the kids would say about me. My mind was racing as to what this meant.

This is no coincidence…God showed up…

That much I knew!

The child services worker listened to the kids for nearly 20 minutes as they shared some of their recent struggles they'd had with their dad. Before leaving she surveyed the home (which was thankfully in order), and promised us that Ahmet would be "put on notice" for his behavior. We could feel safe now. She was recommending that he stay far away from us.

I called my lawyer the next day to share what transpired and he was taken slightly off-guard, but pleasantly so—he thought I was going to say that Ahmet had called DCF on me—as is sometimes the case in bad divorces.

Someone had intervened on our behalf and we felt angels among us since the timing couldn't have been better.

Soon, Ahmet was counseled by his hot-shot lawyer and was court ordered to take an anger management course. Best of all, he was instructed to leave us alone for several months.

No contact.

No threats.

No manipulation.

No drama.

No guilt.

No kidding!

I never did find out who had reported some of the hell he was putting us through. I questioned a friend but she said it wasn't her, so my next guess was that our therapist was required to report it.

Regardless, it was a prayer answered. THANK YOU...that just happened!

Chapter Thirty-One

Step Forward, Give Back

For the first time in quite a while, we were able to let our guard down a notch. It was a much needed liberating wake-up call. Life was happening now—it wasn't waiting until my divorce was final. No matter how uncertain the future, I had to learn to live in the moment. It's all we have. Nothing else is certain.

What can I do to help manifest this peaceful feeling?

Almost immediately I thought of water. I've always loved the water. I love looking at it, being in it, gliding, and the general feeling of it. I can actually swim in it really well too. I'm kind of fish-like, well, a fish that likes chlorine. I'm not too fond of sea creatures.

There's something about just watching water that is very calming to me, especially when it's all placid and smooth. Ever notice a peacefully still lake and then suddenly something nips the surface and causes a rolling ripple effect? Love those ripples in the water too. Sometimes they're slow and gradual, a gentle kiss causing featherlike flutters. Other times the movement is so sudden, it pulsates violently. What I'm trying to say is, the ripples of movement can be slow and calm or they can easily be seen working their course lapping onward through the water. Either way, there's movement.

Forward action equals movement.

Charitable acts are like that. I believe if you perform an act of kindness it sends ripples out into the universe. Sometimes you can clearly see where it goes, other times it's not as noticeable to the visible eye. But either way, a kind act causes far-reaching effects.

During this whole taxing chapter of my life trying to overcome the underhanded, I was extremely blessed to be the recipient of many kind acts. It was time to move forward and give back.

Although I clearly didn't have the means and greens to be radically financially generous, I realized I could give in other ways. I could give my time. Without a full-time job yet I had plenty to give. Showing kindness is as easy as sharing a smile and saying hello.

How many times have you "met" a stranger, maybe an employee at a restaurant or retail shop, and the server had a semi-scowl/super-stressed look on her face? Her look indicates that it's a rough day or time. Maybe she's irritated by her boss, husband, parent, kid, financial situation—whatever, it doesn't matter. You, as the customer, can make or break it.

You can throw some kindness her way, make eye contact, smile, and say something complimentary such as, *"That color looks great on you"* or *"you have amazing eyes."*

I bet if you listen closely you might hear her inhale a tad before you see facial muscles give way to a small smile. She may pause, change her stance, and even stand a little straighter. Forced smile or not, you elicited a positive reaction and very likely changed the way she'll interact with the next customer.

Unless of course the next person barks at her and treats her like crap; then it's back to grumpy girl. And goodbye ripples.

The kids and I tried this approach a few times when we would treat ourselves and go out to eat. During this financially lean period I rediscovered a love for breakfast food—eggs, pancakes, bacon, ham...mmmm. Good stuff.

And cheap.

We started having "breakfast for dinner" at least once a week, and somehow that led us to going to a nearby Denny's restaurant on a Friday night when I didn't want to cook.

There wasn't a single car in the parking lot as we drove up that evening. It was a little unnerving to be honest, but we didn't care.

I guess not many people go to dine at Denny's on a Friday night—before midnight at least.

Well, we were here and it was nice to be out together. We were greeted by an attractive lady who appeared to be around my age, give or take.

Shelby asked for our order and her deep blue eyes were compelling. I started to notice people's eyes and the emotions they held soon after I realized how black and soulless Ahmet's had become. I'd seen them way too bloodshot and unbalanced far too many times.

How did I miss that?

I couldn't quite put my finger on it, but Shelby had a blend of "matter-of-fact-this-is-my-day, ho-hum" with what I thought was a tinge of sadness. Yet there was a sliver of playfulness, too, and she'd light up when talking with the kids.

How and why I came to this conclusion I'm not sure (months later it would be revealed that my initial impression was pretty dead on). That first night we met, from taking our order, I heard a whisper in my head, "Be *extra* kind to her."

The four of us conversed between my son's "all-you-can-eat pancake challenge" and my daughter's "Moons over Miami" whammy. Shelby was attentive and kind, as if we were her only customers.

Okay, so on that particular night we were.

She was especially sweet on Nikole and Tarik and won them over with a fancy coffee treat she concocted just for them. (It could seriously rival a well-known coffee house that charges nearly $5 a cup; I'm just saying.)

After having dinner on the cheap, I ended up leaving a tip that almost mirrored our bill. It just felt right even though I had never done that before.

That night the kids and I had the best time in a long time. Who knew a Denny's could be a haven for us?

We vowed to return and it became "our place." It was nice to go out on a Friday night and not have hordes of people hammering for the latest fix. That Denny's was our special family spot. We even had our very own table in the back right corner where we first met Shelby. We always sat in her station and would talk to her as much as her schedule allowed.

And no matter when we arrived she always seemed to be working.

I took this as another sign that we were meant to be there too.

Time went on and it became more challenging to coordinate two teenagers' schedules. We hadn't been there in a while. One night when Tarik was with his Dad, Nikole and I both felt we should go see her.

We're so glad we did. Shelby lit up when she saw us and said, "You have no idea how happy I am to see you! I was hoping to find you before I left."

I was a little stunned when she mentioned leaving but what struck me right away was the sheer joy and light dancing in her eyes.

"What? Wait? Where are you going?" I asked.

"I wanted to tell you my story but never knew how to begin," she said. "You know how you meet some people and you feel a bond but yet can't bring yourself to share something? Well, I've been serving time in a woman's work-release program. That's why I'm always here, but I just finished my sentence. I get to go home and be with my children and husband."

Whoa, didn't see that one coming!

"Your family brought me such comfort whenever you came in. I have kids their age and I've been missing my own children terribly for the past three years."

A vision of how her eyes looked on the first day we met came back to me: day in, day out—check; sadness—check; there's something you don't know playfulness—check.

Perhaps the most beautiful thing of all is that our friendship wasn't built on me being a good tipper. It was never about that. It was based on two women being brought together, surviving a storm, and sharing a small part of life together. Here we were, both stepping forward and overcoming.

Talk about another "WOW" God moment.

Chapter Thirty-Two

A Helping of Haiti

I was finally springing back to life like a fire-sparkler singeing a dry field. I wanted to keep moving forward since I was suddenly tired of the "one day, some day" world that my life had become.

There were several people I knew from church who were going on a mission trip to Haiti, and I found myself dreaming a wild dream—I wanted to go and be part of it.

What am I crazy? I'm barely holding on.

But with all the craziness that had ensued with the drama of our impending divorce, I found myself reaching out to experience life in ways I hadn't before. Part of the allure of this trip was that we would spend time in a small village and bring love to orphaned children. I really wanted to go and experience this—not only to help those in Haiti, but it would be good for my soul as well.

Being with children makes me happy. I've always felt a pull to try to bring a smile to a little face. It's always my goal to let a child know he/she is special and loved.

Maybe going to Haiti isn't such a crazy idea.

I reached out to friends and family to enlist their support in sponsoring me. While my parents never actually said I was nutso, I kind of think they thought I was. I know they were worried about me and the kids. I sure as heck know how my heart aches when my babies are hurting, and well, I'm their baby no matter how old I get.

I raised the entire amount needed and my parents agreed to stay and watch over Nikole and Tarik while I was gone for the week. This was the first time in a long time that I was excited and passionate about something. I'm not sure exactly what I expected to find on this trip, but I can tell you what I quickly learned.

No matter what the outcome of my divorce, I was rich beyond compare to this part of the world.

If you ever find yourself focusing on what you don't have and are not particularly appreciative for what you do possess, spend some time in a third world country.

Just for a bit. It will totally change your perspective.

After a long bus ride south and then a quick plane, my group of 22 arrived to a very hot and humid Haiti. I thought I knew what hot was having lived in Florida for decades, but whoa! The air was hot soup that melted my face off. It was November.

Oh, I'll never take A/C for granted again!

Hours after landing, we arrived at our humble accommodations by way of one very crowded open-aired taxi bus. With a plethora of potholes and only half a cheek on the torn seat, I got real close to some of my fellow comrade companions. We made our way to the cabin campsite and were given instructions to never leave our shoes uncovered—tarantulas love to settle into warm smelly shoes.

Say what?!

We were also instructed that this was not the week to diet; that we should stock up on carbohydrates to help combat the heat and excessive sweating that would ensure.

Oh, I can totally get onboard with that order.

We attended a local church ceremony that first night. After the worship music ended, I could still hear drums continuing to thump, thump. It was faint, but it was there and others from my group questioned it too.

"Oh, that's from the nearby village," said our leader. "They heard Christians were coming and are casting voodoo spells on you."

Seriously? Oh my...

He said it so nonchalantly that I almost giggled out loud. But yes, we were chanted to sleep by voodoo drums cursing our arrival.

While some adults may have been leery of our presence, the Haitian children welcomed us instantly and warmly. They would grab the hands of the women and girls in our clan and cling to our sides any chance they could—soaking up the love and attention.

Everyone in the village works hard from sunup to sundown. It's a community unit that functions on all members contributing. Most often, younger children are left in the care of older children (even if only older by a few years) so parents and grandparents can work. Work equals survival. It was easy to see why the kids would gravitate toward us mommy figures. They were hungry not only for nourishment but for affection, as well.

We had raised enough money to host two

community rice feedings. This is a spectacular event and a great blessing since each family from the village could receive three gallon-size cans full of uncooked rice. While three cans may not seem like much, it is a time of celebration since this ensures a Haitian family will have food that month. Everyone gathers in the community center and stands patiently in line for his/her turn.

Imagine that...no shoving, pushing, fighting, name calling to be first...and this is for plain rice, not an HD TV, Cabbage Patch doll, or candy bar!

One person from each household comes forward and members of our team count and scoop the rice into the burlap sack, pillowcase, or whatever the villager brought. We offer prayer and ask a blessing as he/she receives the rice. There are many non-Christians in the group, but no one turns down prayer for assistance to help sustain their family.

There was much to see during this eye-opening trip, but two heartbreaking images remain etched in my soul. One was of a very slender elderly man, possibly in his 60s, but it's so hard to tell age. It was midday and he was completely sacked out just outside his wood-woven encampment. At first I thought him directly on the ground—his oversized white tee shirt and denim shorts drooping, but he was perfectly balanced atop two thin bamboo beams.

Geez, my thighs are bigger than both poles combined yet this was his bed.

He looked peaceful though.

The other image I have is of a middle-aged woman. At first glance you'd think she was pregnant, her belly protruding like she was nearing the end of the second trimester. But looking at her weathered face, I could tell she was past child-bearing age. The mass was no baby; rather it was a football-sized tumor. No pain, or at least, bearable pain, equaled no surgery. And surgery was hard to come by so the tumor continued to grow.

She did not look peaceful.

Yes, this was a most enlightening week. There was quiet time for reflection, as well as boisterous times working our butts off in the sun. We had time for kid giggles and silliness, singing, and soccer. There were also times to cry, sometimes privately. I desperately wanted to take each little one home with me. Those sweet little tikes whose eyes flickered with innocence and hope; and the older children, where sparkle has been replaced by sadness and understandings of their plight beginning at around age six.

Why? Why do I live where I do and they live here?

Haiti is not for the weak. And I'm not just talking about the horrid heat and gargantuan tarantulas, which I had five close encounters with; well, five I count. I don't want to dwell on the ones I didn't see in the field at night.

In the United States, while poverty and homelessness exist, everyone in America has access or can get assistance to obtain food, clothes, clean water, doctors, and medicine.

I went to Haiti because I wanted to make a difference in others' lives but I was the one who was touched and came back changed. It may sound cliché, but I realized how rich I was even without a full-time job. I knew that no matter what, all would be all right.

My children and I had boatloads to be thankful for. I had a new sense of peace and calm to me. I will make it through this storm!

Chapter Thirty-Three

Court Day of Reckoning

Question:
How long should a divorce take?
Answer:
It all depends...but less than three years is highly desirable!

I may not be a mathematical whiz, but with the aid of a calculator I know that three years equates to 1,095 days. That's 26,280 hours. It's more than 1.5 million minutes and something like a gazillion seconds. (I don't want to bore you with numbers.)

The point is that's how long I was in marital limbo.

Yes, three long years where time seemed to stand still and creep by.

How and why on earth did it take so long?

Well, I guess it could be said that some men don't divorce well. Not well at all. Especially not Ahmet.

Divorce, while permissible, is still not widely practiced in Turkey or other traditional cultures even today. It doesn't matter if both partners are utterly miserable. And if the marriage was arranged—which is still practiced today, and obviously not just in Turkey—forget it.

Many privileged men, if unhappy, or heck, just

if they want to, can have multiple women to "make them feel better."

Don't worry; I know infidelity exists in America too. If you're a woman in Turkey you're just supposed to deal—and not stray yourself or you'll be blamed.

I'm done dealing; with all the lies, the put-downs, everything.

Ahmet's parents were actually the product of an arranged marriage and while I'm told they loved each other, facial expressions in photos conveyed a different meaning to that line of thinking.

"We all have our crosses to bear."

That was something my grandma would say. I get it now.

Back to my marriage, or rather, the dissolution of it. Given all he had to lose in us, plus his wounded ego, Ahmet did not go down without a fight, nor did he make any of it easy. Mediation proved to be a waste of time and money because he did not own up to the fact that he had at least two other bank accounts—to which he had put one-third of every paycheck for at least the last five years.

I'm sure it's more like, um, our entire marriage.

Call it Mediterranean machismo, but Ahmet felt he was in the right since *he* made all the money. He and his lawyer had many tricks up their sleeves and there was always some way to delay or push the final court day just out of reach.

"Let's take her back to court and lower the alimony and child support. That will get her to fold..."

"I think she's holding out on getting a better job—let's put her through an employability psychological test..."

Ah, Dr. Finney and her three-hour long employability test...what a sad joke that was. She was charged with determining if I was employable.

No shit, lady. I am.

I was honest and told her how Ahmet had encouraged me to stay home for more than half our marriage and that my immediate focus through our divorce was to ensure my kids safety and mental well-being. And with all that he had done to us, it was a full-time job.

Another kicker was that I was working now too. I landed a job at a local newspaper. It just didn't pay all that much. And although I was looking for a higher salaried job, I was not going to take something that left me unavailable to our children.

Ahmet spent nearly $4,000 to have me paper-and-penciled tested by this out-of-touch woman to be told that I was "very polite, intelligent, well-balanced, and employable."

Good job, honey, there's money well spent.

I know Dr. Finney was just doing what she was hired to do but I wanted this sick game over with. No more delays...

One week before our final court date it looked like there might be a delay again. Except there wasn't.

I had my army of family and friends praying for me.

Oh, good Lord, we're going to court and a judge

will decide our fate. Finally!

After three years in the system we were ready to see our second judge and let him settle our finances.

While I wanted to go for full custody, I knew Ahmet would never agree and would drag out our battle even longer. I also knew that I would be the one to continue to raise our kids in the end. He could pretend all he wanted—he wasn't interested in the daily dirty work of parenting. And I was fine with that.

Nikole and Tarik were more than fine with that too.

I had never even been inside a courtroom before this whole sordid experience began. The only image I had were those created by television shows. Court wasn't so daunting anymore. I knew that no matter the outcome of the judge's decision, I would be just fine.

At this stage, I knew that if God loved me enough to have his son die for me, then he would take care of me in any circumstance.

I was in His hands.

During testimony and listening to lawyers and such, I wrote down some fragments of scripture which helped me keep calm. The fact that I was largely at peace during this time still blows me away.

My mom, on the other hand, almost got thrown out by the judge because she was outraged at some of the lies Ahmet's lawyer presented; such as his meager income and support of his family in Turkey.

After her second or third snicker the judge said, "Madame, if you don't remain silent I will have my bailiff escort you out of my courtroom."

I love you, Mom! I'm ok!

She rearranged her seat and positioned herself behind my aunt so the judge couldn't see her mouth move or her fuming facial expressions.

The fact that God allowed me to be confident and composed reaches beyond what I can understand or comprehend. It finally came down to a decision and the judge heard our testimonies and commented that he didn't like Ahmet's perception of what was "his" money during our marriage.

I was awarded the house and, in addition to child support, I would be entitled to receive some alimony for a brief time (based on bogus pay, but whatever).

Ahmet kept what he had sequestered away, letting the kids know they have three houses in Turkey as their inheritance.

But it was done.
Holy crap, we're done!

Chapter Thirty-Four

Free to Dream

Question:
What does it mean when you let someone else dictate your life?
Answer:
It means you'll never find your purpose or have a dream of your own.

I vividly remember thinking during high school, "these four years are dragging by so s-l-o-w-l-y…I just want to graduate and start my life…"

The irony is while I couldn't wait to get to college, I had no idea what would be next. I was unaware that I should start dreaming and planning my life. The thought of dreaming about the future was not a natural part of my cosmic makeup. I guess you could say I lived in the present, which isn't necessarily a bad thing mind you.

It just makes it awkward when you wake up one day and realize you forgot to dream a little dream for yourself.

Or you realize you let someone else dream at your expense...

From the moment we first met well into our marriage, Ahmet had no problem dreaming, scheming, and sharing his vision of the future. He'd own his own shop and retire at 40. When Tarik was little, he started talking about the trips the two of them would take together; vacationing in Turkey, going to bars, drinking, meeting women. Then he'd retire and live six months in the States and six months in Turkey. Half of our family was missing from that pretty little picture he painted— myself and our daughter.

What does that say?

Fast forward. My three-year long divorce is finally behind me. Now that the uncertainty was gone and we were safe, I started seeing a life coach to help me get some groove and balance back to my life. I remember when Julie asked me to discuss my dreams for the future.

"Dreams?"

I must have sounded like an alien mimicking the word as my tone conveyed I was astonished. That one word stopped me in my tracks like a bucket of ice over my head.

Dreams...I forgot I could dream!

I had spent 15 years supporting someone else's dreams and the last three solely focused on surviving. I hadn't even envisioned what life would be like when it was over!

Just hearing the word "dream" coupled with the fact that I had permission to dream, felt so, so liberating...

It was then that I felt I could really take charge and create my own reality. There was no husband to say "no," and nothing to hold me back. I had nothing to fear.

Well, except finances, failure, and fear itself, but heck, I had challenged the devil and won, so look out world, here I come!

But before my dreams could take flight, I needed to go back to basics and figure out some things.

What do I like to do? What comes easily to me?

I struggled with this slightly.

I often just go along with what others like. I know it's where I picked up my fascination with some rock bands, as well as my affinity for shooting pool. I find that bringing someone else happiness makes me happy (part of a "pleaser" personality).

Ah, but there's a fine line in pleasing others and being so chameleon-like that you teeter with co-dependency, destroying yourself in the process.

I know that now.

My second-grade teacher pegged me as a writer after reading a poem I had crafted. I surged with pride. That assignment had come so easily to me while many seemed to struggle and I loved the creating process. I guess you could say I've been a lover of words ever since.

Mine is actually a full-circle kind of story since I had initially started down the path of becoming a journalist in high school and early college. I thought to be a reporter I would have to be cutthroat and aggressive. And let's be honest, my assertiveness skills almost equaled my ability to dream (at the time).

The job I had recently acquired at a local newspaper came by way of faith and what I believe to be divine intervention. I had been asked to write a promotional article for our youth group's hunger awareness campaign. It had been more than a decade since I had written in journalistic format but I accepted the challenge. I prayed before writing that I would do right by our students and the hungry children we were trying to help.

The paper ran the article with nary a word changed. The cherry on top was that it was widely read and well received. Writing this story felt amazing, like I had reconnected my soul.

I needed to do something with writing...

That Christmas when my finances were fading and there were no job prospects in sight, I took some relic writing samples (along with this new piece) and I visited that very same newspaper office. I said I would be willing to freelance, work part time, full time, whatever.

I ended up doing all of that.

The faith of dreaming a little dream and knocking on a door that wasn't yet opened, paved the way for a newfound career in writing. I am hooked. I love sharing someone's special gift, inspiration, and story with the world (or at least my small corner of it).

What dreams do I have for my life?

First, to provide for my children. I'm proud to say we've overcome a great deal of darkness. We're survivors not statistics.

I realize I want to be a voice for oppressed women and children. That in sharing my story it may help others begin to heal—to help them find laughter and humor again and to realize they are not alone and are worthy just the way they are. If you are stuck always looking in the rear view mirror you will never go forward.

    I dream of meeting Ellen DeGeneres and Oprah Winfrey one day (hey, might as well aim high). I plan to keep writing and publishing although I believe my next book should be fictional and fun.

    The story God's writing in me is the greatest story—more than I could ever hope to write alone.

    There is no more "*what now?*"

    It's my life.

    And I'm glad I took it back.

Epilogue

I'm happy to report that I no longer sob in closets or seek them out for solace.

Ahmet has mellowed out considerably since his health has him scared. Stress will do that to you. He has continued to provide well for his children over the years. He even told them they each have a house in Turkey when he dies; ironic how these assets were acquired during our marriage yet weren't split when divorcing.

Oh, well. Forgiving is letting God deal with the person/problem.

Nikole and Tarik are in college now blazing their own future and path in life. They have grown up so beautifully and are amazing. They each have a heart for helping children and speaking of God's love. My children are my strength and inspiration for reclaiming my life, for I had to fight to make their future better, as well.

Ahmet has a tenuous relationship with his children. It's not as frequent or friendly as he'd like (or feels he deserves), but he has one—because of Nikole and Tarik's grace in forgiving him. He is still callous with his words, but he has learned to stifle his anger (mostly).

We have been schooled to "establish boundaries," as our therapists like to call it. Now that they are both over 18 years of age, I don't have to see him, and avoidance works just fine for me.

Every so often Ahmet tries to cross that

boundary with me and gets frustrated that I don't allow him that control (most of the time—life's a work in progress). He's often tried to sway the kids by saying, "Your mom and I are good now" or "She's a close friend."

But they know better.

I told them from the beginning that I would always try to show their father respect, for without him, they would not be here. And though I have made mistakes and have regrets, my life unfolded the way it was meant to—they are my beautiful children.

I can be friendly with their dad, but he is not my friend. He once was, and that friendship led to marriage and then parenthood. But he lost the trust of my friendship long ago.

A friend loves and respects and holds you up— friends do not lie, devalue, or destroy.

I've grown up a lot during this journey of paradoxes. I was strengthened through my weakness. I received through giving.

And I gained by losing.

I am excited about my future and next steps. This book has been a labor of love that has been hard to write at times but has provided additional healing.

If I can make it through the storm, I know it is within you to overcome the underhanded as well.

You are not alone on your journey, my friend.

If I Knew Then What I Know Now...

You're still reading? Awesome!

This may interest you. After previewing my first draft, I sat down with my friend to debrief over pancakes and coffee (love breakfast food, have I said that?). We got through the mechanics, edits, and such and then she paused before she said, "Suzan, you're a smart, intelligent, attractive woman, how did you...why were you..."

I cut her off cold, "completely pathetic?" I figured my weaknesses were out there anyway so no sense trying to be delicate about it.

She wanted to know if I knew what had made me so susceptible to my ex-husband and suggested I include a "lessons learned" chapter or share advice for other women, mothers, and daughters.

I loved that idea and here it goes from the heart. Please keep in mind I am not a licensed mental health practitioner, nor am I an expert on emotional abuse. I did conduct some research for writing this book and encourage you to explore more on your own as well.

First, you may be experiencing emotional abuse if someone:

• Continually criticizes, embarrasses, bullies, or humiliates you

• Is always right and puts you down in a way that

144

makes you doubt yourself

• Does not trust you and acts jealous or possessive

• Discourages you from seeing friends or family; isolates you from others

• Monitors where you go, who you call and who you spend time with

• Does not want you to work

• Controls finances or refuses to share bank information or money

• Expects you to ask permission for all you spend or do

• Punishes you by withholding affection or giving you the "silent treatment"

• Threatens to hurt you, the children, your family, or your pets

• Makes you feel controlled, isolated, intimidated, or exhausted

None of these signs alone prove that you're in an unhealthy relationship by any means. But, if you can put a check next to a number of them or have read along and thought to yourself, "Holy shit I can relate," then my advice to you is to please sit up and take notice.

Going back, I would not have ignored some very telling warning signs, such as:

• Conversation should be two-ways. If it's hugely one-sided and you're not asked to share your opinion or even speak, could be your partner is a bit of a narcissist.

• If you confront your partner about something

he said/did that you find out about and he blatantly lies to you or dismisses it as "a little thing," you have big problems.

• Do not ignore gaps or changes in time and pay attention to stories that change or get modified—it's a good indicator of being lied to.

• Cultural and religious differences can grow over time.

• Being nervous to bring up a certain topic or afraid to share your own preferences is not a healthy response.

• If your partner's rage worries you and you fear "setting him off" then it is likely you are in an abusive relationship.

• Finally, ask yourself, if you don't trust your partner to be truthful and you are not being shown respect, why are you staying?

If you know someone who may be in an emotionally abusive relationship, here are some suggestions from me to you:

• Listen and be aware of the warning signs of abuse. Yours, and your friend's safety, should always be top of mind.

• Don't be afraid to reach out and check in on your friend.

• Repeat as necessary. It may not be obvious, but a mentally-abused woman is often very isolated and feels alone.

• Do not be discouraged if your advice is not taken. Much like a smoker or someone who's overweight, you can't force a person to seek help. It's her journey, her timetable, and she will when she's ready.

• Or she won't.

• Avoid being judgmental.

• Do not stop reaching out. Offer to get together. Walks and phone calls are great encouragement for those financially strapped.

• Pray for her. If she is not a Christian and you are, consider inviting her to your church. The power of prayer and God is amazing.

• Connection is an incredibly empowering tool. Thank you for being a friend.

4 Things I've learned along the way:

• I am not worthless.

• I am loved.

• I am forgiven.

• I am not alone.

THANK YOU

Thank you for your time and support. I would love to hear from you—the good, the bad, and the ugly!

Overcoming the Underhanded: The True Story of a Life Reclaimed deals with issues of mental abuse, alcoholism, depression, financial infidelity, divorce, culture, and religion.

If there is one takeaway from reading my story, it is my heartfelt prayer that you recognize you are not alone in any struggle you may have. We are here together, and we are connected and can support each other.

Feel free to share or loan your book to someone you think may benefit from hearing my story (or buy them a copy of their own). I love hearing how people are paying it forward!

Leave a Review

If you enjoyed the book (and to be clear, I know it does not mean you enjoyed what my children and I went through—I get that a lot) please consider writing a book review on Amazon or Goodreads. You do not need to provide your real name (example: "Amazon Reader" or Sue K.).

About the Author

Suzan E. Zan is an award-winning author who is passionate about encouraging others to find their voice. A creative at heart with a heart for humanity, she infuses humor and playfulness in her writings, whether poetry, non-fiction, news articles, or blogs.

With a penchant for sharing sass and soul, this author loves to entertain while drawing you in with her "keep it real" voice. Suzan writes to heal and inspire and exposes the "hard places and spaces" and has a knack for sharing heartache with humor.

Her debut book, "Overcoming the Underhanded: The True Story of a Life Reclaimed," is her memoir about emotional abuse, gaslighting, marriage, religion, culture, alcoholism, and healing. Told with humor. Really.

How to Reach Suzan E. Zan:
Here are some ways you can connect with me:
- Website: http://bit.ly/SuzanZan
- Facebook: SuzanZan369
- Twitter: @SuzanZan369
- Email: SuzanZan369@gmail.com
- Phone: 850-629-9857
- Amazon:
https://www.amazon.com/author/suzanzan

Resources:

The National Domestic Violence Hotline:
800-799-7233 | www.thehotline.org
Office of Women's Health Hotline:
800-994-9662 | www.womenshealth.gov
Narcissistic Personality Disorder:
https://www.mayoclinic.org/diseases-
conditions/narcissistic-personality-disorder/symptoms-
causes/syc-20366662
Gaslighting:
http://www.thehotline.org/what-is-gaslighting/
Al-Anon/Alateen:
https://al-anon.org/

www.ingramcontent.com/pod-product-compliance
Lightning Source LLC
Chambersburg PA
CBHW060859280326
41934CB00007B/1109